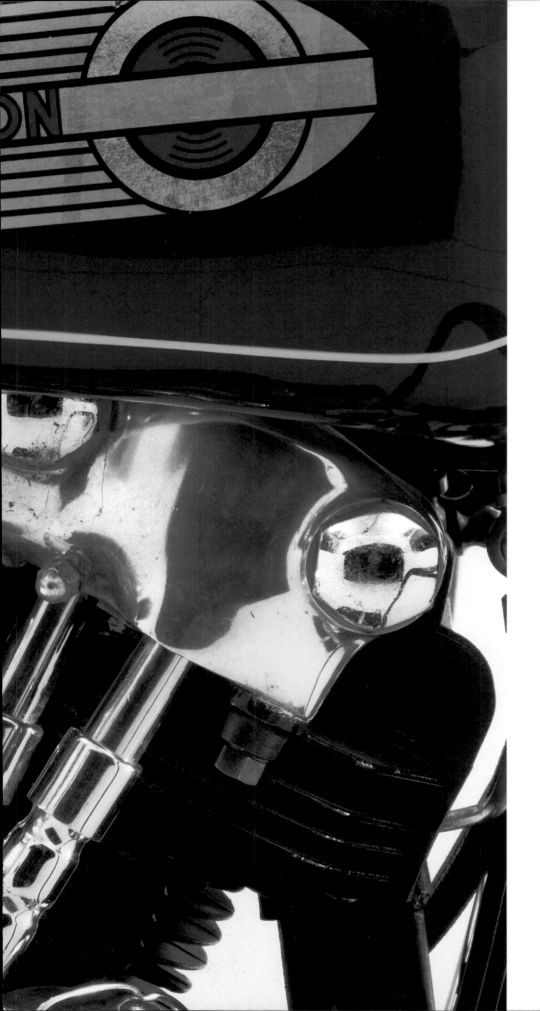

THE HARLEY-DAVIDSON MOTOR CO.

ARCHIVE COLLECTION

RANDY LEFFINGWELL AND **DARWIN HOLMSTROM**

PHOTOGRAPHY BY
RANDY LEFFINGWELL

FOREWORD BY
BILL DAVIDSON

motorbooks

The Harley-Davidson Archives Collection contains more than motorcycles alone. From handwritten articles of incorporation and meeting minutes written at the kitchen table to service bulletins from the very early years of the company, the document collection alone totals millions of pages. Early advertising and engineering photographic images and negatives number well over one hundred thousand. The collection also contains countless pieces of motorcycle memorabilia, riding apparel, pins, trophies, advertising materials, signage, and the list goes on.

As a result, cataloging and researching these items is an ongoing effort, employing the skills of full-time professional archivists as well as graduate student interns. With each day, the mining of this vast collection of historic information reveals more and more accurate details regarding the company's history, and the evolution of its products. This book provides the reader with the best information we have available today. The Harley-Davidson Museum in Milwaukee houses temporary exhibit space with ever-changing themes and topics. Come visit and experience an ever evolving story as it unfolds.

First published in 2008 by MBI Publishing Company and Motorbooks, an imprint of MBI Publishing Company, 400 First Avenue North, Suite 300, Minneapolis MN 55401 USA

The information in this book is true and complete to the best of our knowledge. All recommendations are made without any guarantee on the part of the author or Publisher, who also disclaim any liability incurred in connection with the use of this data or specific details.

The Publisher recognizes, further, that some words, model names, and designations mentioned herein are the property of the trademark holder. We use them for identification purposes only.

Motorbooks titles are also available at discounts in bulk quantity for industrial or sales-promotional use. For details write to Special Sales Manager at MBI Publishing Company, 400 First Avenue North, Suite 300, Minneapolis, MN 55401 USA.

To find out more about our books, join us online at www.motorbooks.com.

ISBN-13: 978-0-7603-3184-2

Editor: Darwin Holmstrom
Designer: Tom Heffron

Printed in China

Published by Motorbooks, an imprint of MBI Publishing Company,
under license from Harley-Davidson Motor Company.

CONTENTS

FOREWORD

A walk down the aisle of any bookstore in any city throughout the world reveals the extent to which the history of the Harley-Davidson Motor Company has been chronicled. This includes the impact our motorcycles have had on America and other places around the globe. Harley-Davidson is one of the most recognized brands in the world and the only American survivor out of hundreds of motorcycle companies that had their start in the early to mid-1900s.

This book is a departure from the plethora of previously published articles and histories of our company and our product, for it is the first-ever look inside the Harley-Davidson corporate Archives vehicle collection. Thanks to the vision of William, Walter, and Arthur Davidson and William Harley, this company (and in fact this fantastic collection) still exists after one hundred years. The company founders began saving at least one motorcycle from each model year beginning in 1915, and this practice continues to this day.

The Archives vehicle collection now numbers over 460 motorcycles ranging from 1903 to the present, many of which (from 1915 to present) were taken directly from the assembly line and entered into the collection. In 1919, the founders advertised locally to re-purchase vehicles from both dealers and riders to fill the gap between 1903 and 1915. This makes it the only collection of its kind in the world. The collection also contains special-interest vehicles obtained from collectors and private parties over time.

Going back to my earliest childhood memories, I can't remember a day when Harley-Davidson motorcycles were not a part of my life. As soon as my feet could reach the footpegs, I became a rider and have been riding ever since. That's a great thing about this company; we ride what we build. And we ride with our loyal customers, dealers, and employees, sharing products and a culture that has grown and prospered for over one hundred years.

This book has given me the opportunity to reflect on just how far we have come. Each of the images in this book is a chapter in the life of the Motor Company, from the atmospheric-valve, belt-driven singles of the very early days to the blistering performance of a V-Rod drag bike setting another track record today. Harley-Davidson provided vehicles that served in two world wars and survived the Great Depression. It took human imagination to design and human hands to build these motorcycles, dealers to sell and service them, and, of course, people to ride them, people that to this day we refer to as "enthusiasts." This book is a tribute to all those who helped build a truly great motorcycle, a great company, and a great brand.

I am frequently asked what I think separates a Harley-Davidson motorcycle from other motorcycles. The answer is that nothing looks, sounds, or feels like a Harley. Yet it goes deeper than that. No other motorcycle embodies the history or soul of a Harley-Davidson. No other brand incorporates the spirit of the American dream—the freedom, the independence, or the adventure. If Harley-Davidson did not exist, I feel the world would be a very different place.

I'd like to thank our riders and our worldwide dealer network, people whose passion and support have made all this possible, for their commitment to motorcycling and our brand.

This book contains only a part of the collection now housed in the Harley-Davidson Museum in Milwaukee—just a stone's throw away from where it all began in 1903. It is your museum and a tribute to the Harley-Davidson family of riders, dealers, and employees. I hope you can join us in Milwaukee to visit the museum.

See you on the road; all the best.

ENJOY!

Bill Davidson

—Bill Davidson
Vice President, Core Customer Marketing

INTRODUCTION

The Harley-Davidson Motor Co.
Archive Collection

Many of us have heard the rags-to-riches history of one of the most revered motorcycle marques in the world, Harley-Davidson. We've heard the story of three Davidsons and a Harley starting the company in a backyard shed and building three vehicles back in 1903. Much of the early history of the company is the subject of conjecture and speculation, but some things we know for sure.

During the last century there were more than 150 domestic motorcycle manufacturers in the United States, 7 of which were located in Milwaukee, Wisconsin, the same city in which Harley and the Davidsons began building motorcycles. As with most industries in their infancy, the majority of these motorcycle companies were short lived, either due to undercapitalization or to an inability to develop a distribution network and market, and then consistently serve that market. Harley-Davidson had sufficient capital and was able to develop an outstanding distribution network and market.

By 1920, Harley-Davidson had become the largest motorcycle manufacturer in the world, and by 1953, there were just two American motorcycle manufacturers left standing: Harley-Davidson and Indian, based in Springfield, Massachusetts. That same year Indian closed its doors. Today, Harley-Davidson corporate offices occupy the same buildings that began as the Juneau Avenue factory, which are just a stone's throw away from the location of the original shed.

From the very beginning, all things Harley-Davidson came from Milwaukee. By 1973, when vehicle manufacturing moved to York, Pennsylvania, more than 1.25 million motorcycles had been built and shipped from this site. The Juneau Avenue complex, as it is now called, is listed in the National Register of Historic Places.

Housed in the 3800 Building is the Harley-Davidson Archives, a 3,100-square-foot area containing the company history in the form of historic corporate documents, literature dating back to 1905, service manuals, owner manuals, tens of thousands of images and photographic negatives, point-of-sale and advertising materials, dealer correspondence, rider apparel, and all manner of Harley-Davidson collectibles. This collection creates a rare historic timeline, preserved from the very early years of the company.

A separate space houses the vehicle collection, and above the padlocked gate, a sign reads: "Through this gate pass the oldest and greatest motorcycles in the world!" That's what this book is all about: the Harley-Davidson vehicle collection. It's the first comprehensive look into the only collection of its kind in the world.

Many have speculated over the years about why the vehicle collection was started, a question for which there is no concrete explanation. Whatever the reason, the fact remains that it does exist, and it includes more than 460 vehicles. The core of the collection consists of vehicles from 1915—the year the collection was started—to the present.

Most of these vehicles were taken directly from the production line and, in some instances, may have been engineering prototypes or test units. Vehicles from 1914 back to 1905 were actually re-purchased, either from owners or dealers in the field. To this day, at least one vehicle from each model year takes its place within the collection.

There are special-interest vehicles, as well as a Harley-Davidson boat, snowmobiles, golf cars, police vehicles, and prototype models that never saw their way to production. There are special, one-off customs used for advertising or dealer point of sale.

No other motor vehicle manufacturer had the foresight to save what Harley-Davidson has saved for more than one hundred years. The archival artifacts chronicle more than just Harley-Davidson history; they represent the evolution of technology, styling, advertising, and product development. Most important, however, is that the collections reflect the lives of those who built, sold, and rode a true American legend.

To dealers and riders of yesterday as well as today, thank you for keeping the legend alive.

The process of vehicle conservation can at times be somewhat tedious, with literally weeks spent in cleaning one cylinder and similar time spent in conserving original sheet metal with its varnish top coat. Yet every once in a while, as we disassemble an early model, the past speaks to us. One such moment recently occurred while disassembling a 1925 JD that had not had a wrench put to it for more than 80 years. As the tank halves were unbolted, it became a rather solemn moment. It required two pairs of hands, and you can imagine our reaction when the tanks were split, revealing a clear, distinct thumbprint on the inside-left tank half. There were a couple of trial stripes on the inside as well. One can't help but wonder who the person behind this thumbprint was. How old was he? Was he married? Did he have children? For an instant, we were taken back to another time and briefly touched the hand that was the first to assemble this piece of history.

The Harley-Davidson Museum

Since the very beginning, Harley-Davidson has been located and headquartered in a part of Milwaukee, Wisconsin, known as Concordia/Merrill Park, the latter named after one of the early city fathers. The famous "shed" was located on the southwest corner of what is now 38th Street and Highland Boulevard. When

you consider the fact that at the turn of the last century, there were many other domestic motorcycle manufacturers, it is amazing that only Harley-Davidson has survived. As we reflect on the last hundred-plus years, one asks why all the others didn't make it. What formula did Harley-Davidson have that the others lacked? The simple answer is that the company provided a dealer organization that met customer needs, be those needs for sales, service, or socialization. Each dealership had and has its own personality and unique atmosphere. Today, as always, Harley-Davidson dealers are as much enthusiasts as the customers they serve. They too ride, race, and love Harley-Davidson motorcycles.

The individuals who comprise Harley-Davidson management were and are great savers of everything pertaining to the business, and in the Harley-Davidson Archives resides literature dating back to 1905, as well as more than 100,000 negatives and images dating back to the early days of the company. The Archives also houses advertising pieces that chronicle the design and development of Harley-Davidson products to this day, miles of early racing and motorcycle club event footage, vintage clothing and race gear, trophies, awards, signs, clocks, and AMA memorabilia, not to mention more than 450 motorcycles beginning with Serial Number One, the first V-twin from 1909, military vehicles, police vehicles, dragsters, factory customs, and prototypes, all part of a rich heritage.

1909
First V-Twin Engine

This Model 5-D represents the
first V-Twin vehicle produced by
Harley-Davidson. It was available in
Renault Gray or Piano Black. The
7 horsepower motor incorporated
magneto ignition. The engine
configuration began a chapter of
company history that now spans
more than 94 years as it is
still the centerpiece of vehicle design
to this day. This vehicle is the only one
known to exist.

INTRODUCTION | 9

The Harley-Davidson Vehicle Collection:
Care and Preservation

The Harley-Davidson vehicle collection is actually composed of three distinct groups of motorcycles: the core collection, vehicles from 1914 back to Serial Number One, and vehicles purchased from collectors and restorers around the world to fill holes in the collection.

The core collection consists of at least one model from each model year beginning in 1915. As required, these motorcycles are disassembled, and each piece is meticulously cleaned by hand using non-abrasive cleaning agents so as not to degrade original pinstriping or other cosmetic details like decals and appliqués. At no time are parts re-plated, painted, or replaced. Items that deteriorate over time, such as rubber handgrips, tires, and seats, are replaced as required, although the vast majority of the collection vehicles retain these original items.

The vehicles from 1914 back to Serial Number One, excluding the 1909 twin, were purchased by the Motor Company from riders or from dealer inventory, probably in 1919. Some of these machines have been modified in some minor ways, but otherwise they have been retained in the collection in the same condition as originally acquired. As with the core collection, these vehicles have been disassembled, cleaned, and re-assembled. Serial Number One was restored for the company's celebration of its 95th anniversary. The 1909 twin was retained from the original production run and is completely original.

The last group of vehicles consists of those purchased to fill holes in the collection. Were we to have saved one of each model vehicle from each model year, several buildings the size of our Juneau Avenue facilities would be required to house them, so vehicles in the core collection were usually those deemed historically significant at the time of their manufacture. Over time, other vehicles that weren't previously selected have attained historic significance. When a vehicle is later deemed important to the collection, Archives acquires the best available example of that vehicle. These acquisitions, if not accurately restored, are completely disassembled. Proper finishes and plating are then applied, incorrect parts are replaced, and the vehicle is reassembled. The Archive collection of photographs, manuals, bills of materials, and same-era reference vehicles ensure the accuracy of the restoration. As a rule of thumb, full restoration is only used as a last resort, for *a vehicle is original only one time, yet can be restored many times.*

Motorcycles like King Kong, the Rhinestone FLH, and the 1939 and 1955 Servi-Cars, for example, have been kept in their as-acquired condition, receiving only superficial cleaning. To restore these vehicles would remove the patina acquired over time, and they would no longer be original.

"Untouched for 82 Years"

The Harley-Davidson Archives vehicle collection is currently housed in a 94-year-old building within the Juneau Avenue complex. Known as the "3800 Building," it had been used for American Lightweight production from 1948 to 1966. Prior to that, the 3800 Building housed single-cylinder engine, transmission, and vehicle production. It also served as the center for shipping and for spare-parts storage. In a way, the building itself is somewhat of a time capsule, complete with ceiling brackets that held shafts and wood pulleys to drive leather belts that ran lathes, drill presses, and milling machines. The concrete steps are worn concave, evidence of those who came before us and who worked their craft in the early years of the company.

The document collection itself dates back to 1903 and consists of millions of pages, including customer communications with the factory as well as personal diaries and scrapbooks, a true mosaic of the company's early development. The Archives collections house the company history, dealer history, and most important, rider history. For, in the end, were it not for loyal Harley-Davidson customers from the very beginning, this book would not have been possible.

To celebrate the company, the dealers, and the riders, the Harley-Davidson Museum was conceived and designed as a fitting place to house the collections, and in what better location than the place where it all began: Milwaukee, Wisconsin. The museum is located on a 20-acre parcel of land at the corner of Sixth and Canal Streets near downtown Milwaukee and features vintage and special-interest motorcycles and related memorabilia, as well as a restaurant, café, retail shop, meeting space, special events facilities, and the company archives. The total square footage of the museum complex is approximately 130,000 square feet and includes both permanent and temporary exhibit space.

In the museum, visitors will be able to view motorcycles from every model year, right up to the present day. Early racing exhibits will show how important racing was in the early days of the company, and how the saying "Race on Sunday, Sell on Monday" came about as a result of the popularity of racing in the teens, 1920s, and 1930s. In those days, racing was the best form of advertising for Harley-Davidson dealers nationwide. And the rivalry between Indian and Harley-Davidson drew huge crowds until Indian closed its doors. Exhibits will provide visitors with a snapshot of Harley-Davidson's vehicle support of allied

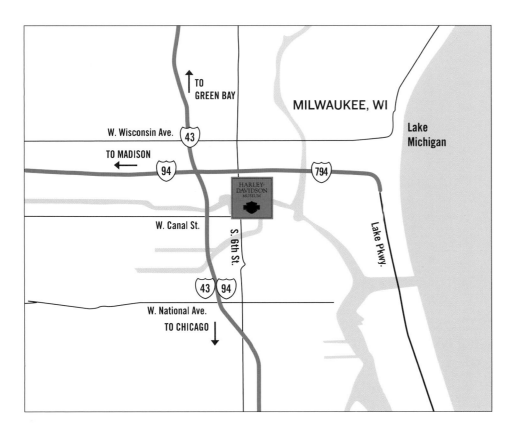

troops in two world wars and include a special model XS designed for use in North Africa, a vehicle featured in this book.

Visitors to the museum will experience the Motor Company's role as a creator of American folk art when viewing early "bobbers" and the "Billy" and "Captain America" reproductions from the cult-classic movie *Easy Rider*. They will be reminded of how important police vehicles have been to our society from the teens to the present. Through letters, scrapbooks, and diaries, they will relive the experiences of dealers and riders from the now-distant past and better understand why Harley-Davidson is a survivor.

Exhibits will take visitors through the merger of the company with AMF in 1969 and follow that 11-year association until 1981, when the company returned to private ownership. The early 1980s marked a time when the balance could have gone either way, and Harley-Davidson could have become nothing more than a memory. As we all know, that didn't happen, and through these exhibits visitors will experience the Motor Company's triumphant rebirth in the 1980s.

With each decade depicted in the museum exhibits, visitors can begin to understand part of the Harley-Davidson mystique. It obviously means different things to different people, but at its heart is the venerable V-twin, with its unique sound, architecture, and low center of gravity that provide the distinctive Harley-Davidson riding experience—an experience shared by millions of enthusiasts worldwide. Hardcore outlaw bikers, the retired couple with their sidecar rig, and all Harley riders in between carry on the greatest sport on earth. To all of you, and our dealers, this is your book.

This book is the first in-depth look inside the corporate Archives, and yet it embodies a mere fraction of the extensive collections housed at the museum site. So we sincerely hope that this presentation whets your appetite for a trip to Milwaukee in the not-too-distant future as you come to realize that the company founders had it right all the time—Milwaukee is the place to be.

1

"The Silent Gray Fellows"

Early Singles and Twins: 1903–1914

As the United States entered the twentieth century, mechanical marvels promised to revolutionize the everyday lives of its citizens. Optimism defined the era, and optimism drove a new breed of entrepreneur: people who harnessed their ingenuity, resourcefulness, and willingness to engage in hard work in an effort to create a better world.

The results of such efforts led directly to the founding of the Harley-Davidson Motor Company. During the first two decades of the twentieth century, Harley-Davidson rose from among the hundreds of other such companies producing motorized bicycles and motorcycles to become the world's preeminent motorcycle manufacturer. In the process, the company manufactured motorcycles that today are recognized as fine examples of industrial art.

1903 Serial Number One

This 1903 Harley-Davidson motorcycle bears serial number "1," at least in part. After totally disassembling the machine for restoration in 1996–1997, Archives staff discovered the number "1" stamped on several components, such as the flywheel, carburetor, and fork stem. But other components were manufactured at a later date. The frame, for example, is believed to have been built sometime after midyear 1905 because it has a sidecar lug under the steering head.

During the 1996–1997 restoration, Archives staff learned this motorcycle had been built for competition because it featured a higher-than-normal compression ratio. At that time, the staff fabricated period-correct handlebars and a seat post to replace the incorrect pieces on the bike, which dated from at least 1908. This single-cylinder engine originally displaced 24.74 cubic inches, or 405 cubic centimeters, with bore and stroke of 3x3 1/2 inches, but the cylinder on this example has been bored to 3 1/8 inches. The main crankcase bushings are brass. The connecting rod has the number "55" stamped in it. A total-loss dry-cell battery system provides ignition spark. Pedals and a chain start the engine and assist in climbing hills. A flat leather belt transmits engine power to the rear wheel. The motorcycle weighs 180 pounds.

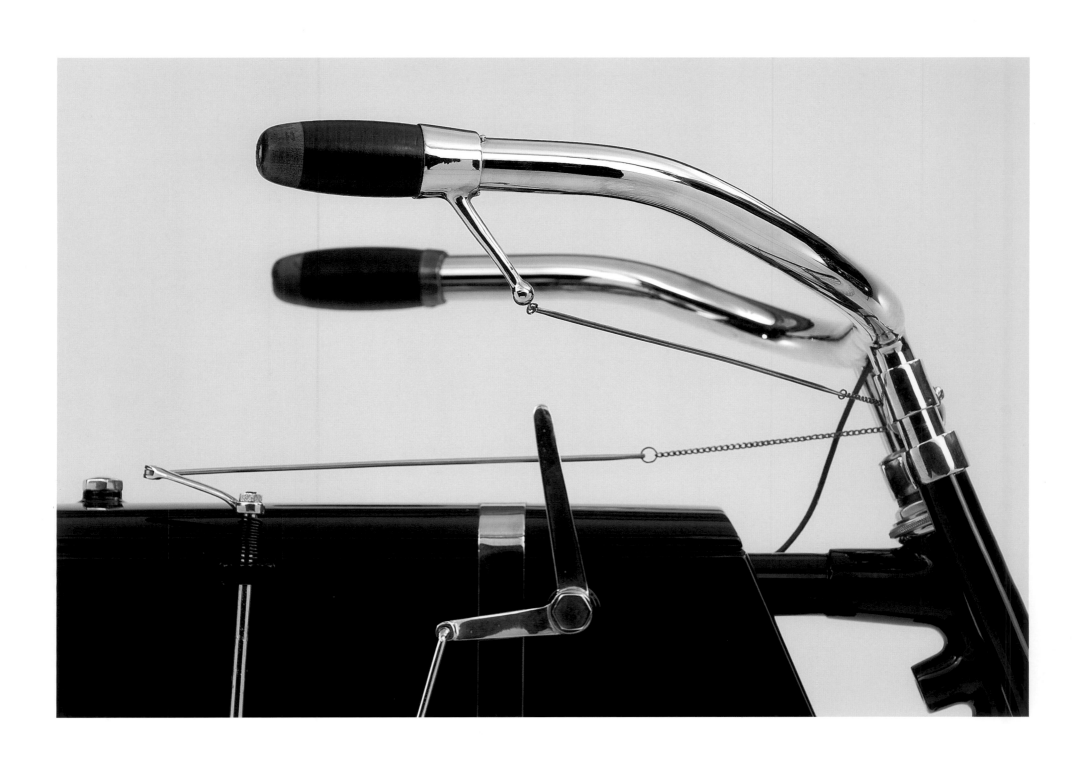

1906 Single

This 1906 single is one of 50 singles the Motor Company manufactured in 1906. This was an early restoration. The gas tank and handlebars appear to come from a 1908 model. The lettering on the tank is larger than the original 1906 lettering. It retains the 26.8-cubic-inch engine used on earlier models. This example has a broken fin on the bottom left side of the cylinder. A bicycle-type rear coaster brake handles stopping duties. The wheelbase is 51 inches, and the tank holds 1.5 gallons of gasoline plus 2 quarts of oil. Total weight is about 185 pounds.

Harley-Davidson sold these machines for $200 in 1906. The bottom of the front fork should be nickel plated. This example wears Piano Black paint, but Harley-Davidson introduced a second color called Renault Gray in 1906.

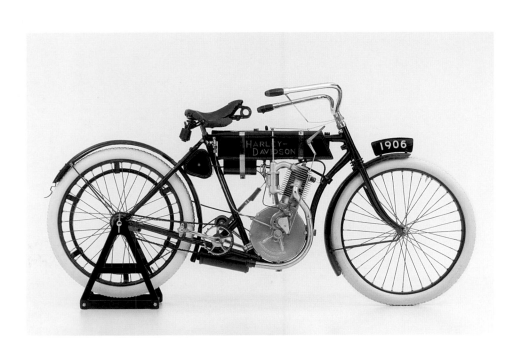

1907 Single

Harley-Davidson Motor Company production tripled in 1907, and the company manufactured 150 of these singles in either Renault Gray (shown here) or Piano Black. Records indicate that the Motor Company acquired this motorcycle for display, and it apparently was repainted sometime after 1908. The front fork head has the Bar & Shield logo affixed to it, although this logo was not used on vehicles until 1910.

The base price rose 5 percent from the previous year, to $210. That extra $10 bought the purchaser improved riding comfort, thanks to the technologically advanced Sager-style cushion front fork with helical coil springs in the parallel tubes.

Pedals and chain still started the 26.8-cubic-inch single, and a flat leather belt still drove the rear wheel. Engineering enlarged the flywheel diameter to 10 inches.

Gasoline capacity remained at 1.5 gallons, giving riders a range of 100 to 125 miles. Oil capacity grew to 2.5 quarts, providing 500 miles of lubrication. Tire width expanded to 2.5 inches, though wheel diameter remained 28 inches. This example has a Persons seat, a hand-operated muffler cutout, polished cases, and a battery box for the three dry-cell batteries. When the company re-acquired this motorcycle, both handgrips were missing, and technicians replaced them and the rear axle with reproduction pieces.

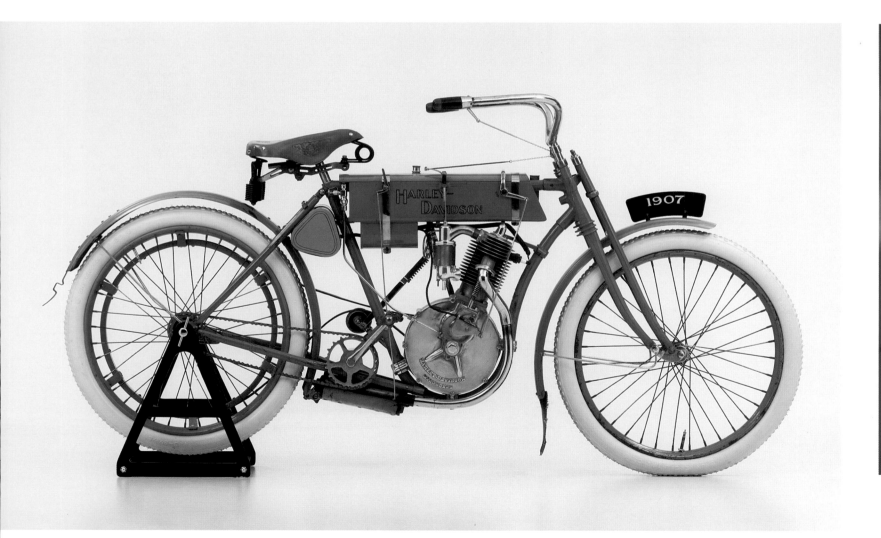

1909 Model 5-D

This is the only known example of Harley-Davidson's first production V-twin motorcycle. It featured a new 7-horsepower, 45-degree twin-cylinder engine set in a V configuration, with 3x3 1/2-inch bore and stroke and a magneto ignition. Total displacement measured 50 cubic inches (810.83 cubic centimeters). A flat belt or an optional V-belt drove the rear wheel. The company carried over the pedal-and-chain starting system.

Like all Harley-Davidson engines up until that time, the new V-twin used the DeDion-Bouton atmospheric intake valves. The descending piston sucked the intake valve open, allowing the air-fuel mixture to enter the engine. Archives records indicate that this system did not work well in tests, and the company discontinued it immediately. Manufacturing assembled 27 of these models, all recalled to the factory. This example shows considerable evidence of having been disassembled many times; Archives staff members presume it served as some kind of test vehicle for engineering.

This frame is slightly heavier and longer (60 inches compared with 56) than the single. It has a heavier, wider front fork. The company equipped this motorcycle with a Troxel saddle, hand-operated muffler cutout, right-hand throttle, and left-hand spark advance.

This example is painted Renault Gray with Carmine striping (which is fading), although the company also offered the bike in Piano Black. All bright parts are nickel plated over copper. The aluminum casing is polished. The Motor Company set a price of $325 for these first-ever H-D twins.

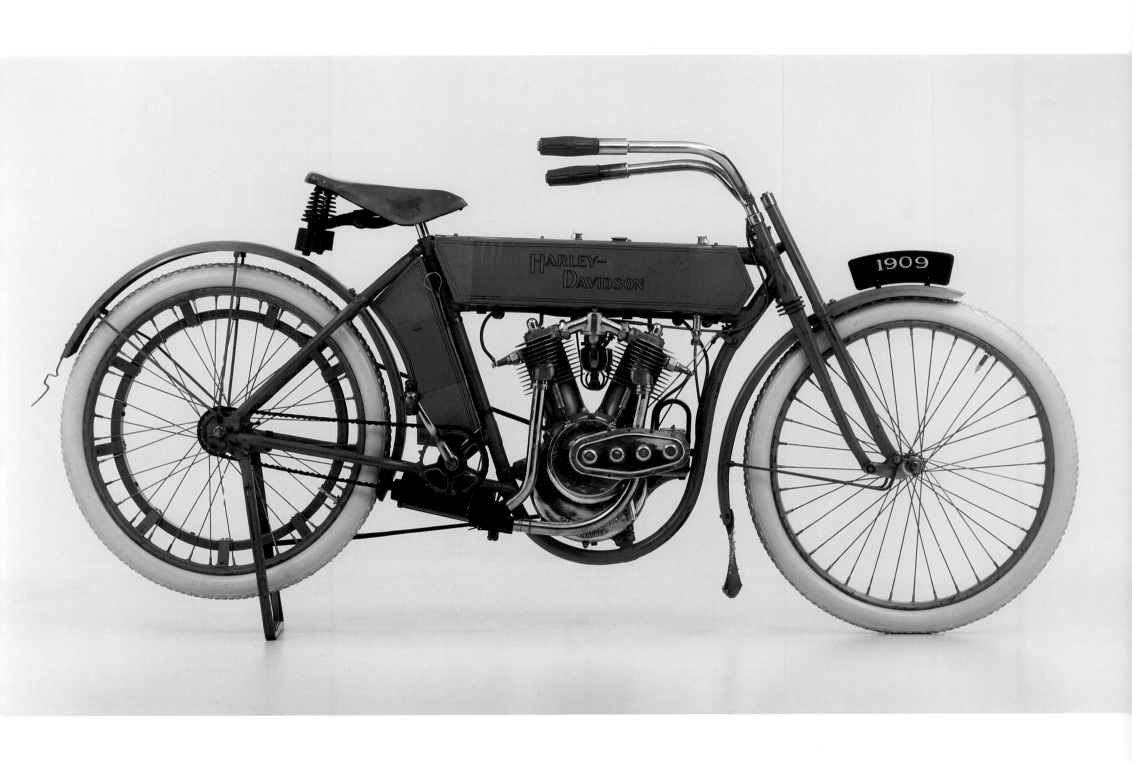

1909 Model 5 Single

This 1909 Model 5 single appears to have several prototype components, most notably a 3.5-quart oil tank concealed under the gas tank. A new-for-1909 30-cubic-inch engine with bore and stroke of 3.3125x4 inches provided riders with 4-plus horsepower in the Model 5 single. Engineering intended the new engine and its increased horsepower output to address the earlier shortcomings in urban and rural hill-climbing capabilities.

This model introduced a redesigned, longer gas tank to better fill the space in the frame. The company also provided a standard centerstand and an improved cushion front fork with larger tubing. The toolbox was moved under the battery box. Harley-Davidson manufactured 864 of the Model 5s in 1909, selling them for $210.

1910 Model 6 Single

This 1910 Model 6 still has the three original 1.5-volt dry-cell batteries for the total-loss ignition system wired in series inside the battery box. It appears that the Motor Company retained this motorcycle from new because records indicate that this motorcycle has had at least two different freewheeling clutch assemblies fitted for evaluation. One configuration used a hand clutch on the handlebars, while the other used a lever on the side of the tank.

In 1910, the 4-horsepower, 30-cubic-inch single used new cylinder barrels with more cooling fins. This was the final year for radial cooling fins on the cylinder head. A belt idler mechanism allowed the rider to stop the motorcycle without killing the engine. The idler assembly is missing on this example. To improve power transmission to the rear wheel, engineering widened the flat leather belt from 1.5 to 1.75 inches. They also shortened the wheelbase from 56 to 55 inches. Engineering enlarged gasoline capacity from 6 to 7 quarts but reduced oil capacity slightly from 3 1/2 to 3 quarts, though advertising copy still claimed a lubrication range of between 600 and 800 miles.

This bike features a right-hand spark advance and left-hand throttle, as well as a hand-operated muffler cut-out. The saddle is a Troxel. Factory production staff polished all aluminum parts. They manufactured 2,302 of these motorcycles in 1910, selling them for $210 apiece.

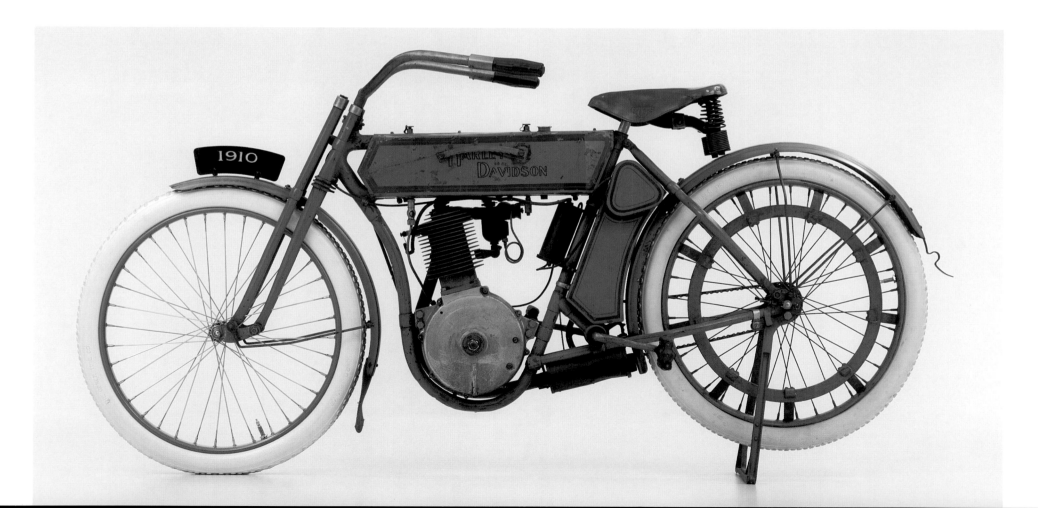

1911 Model 7-A

Engineering redesigned the motorcycle frame in 1911, changing the front frame down-tube to straight from its previous S-curve design. One effect of this change was to provide riders with a lower seating position. In addition, engineering replaced the horizontal fins on the cylinder head with vertical fins. On this example, the front belt sprocket is incomplete, and the idler assembly is missing. It has a Troxel saddle, left-hand spark advance, right-hand throttle, and hand-operated muffler cut-out.

Engineering enlarged gas tank capacity from 1 3/4 gallons to 2 gallons and returned to the 3 1/2-quart oil tank. Total Harley-Davidson motorcycle production reached 5,625 in 1911, though the number of 7-A models produced is uncertain. The Model 7-A sold new for $250, $25 more than the battery-ignition version of the Model 7.

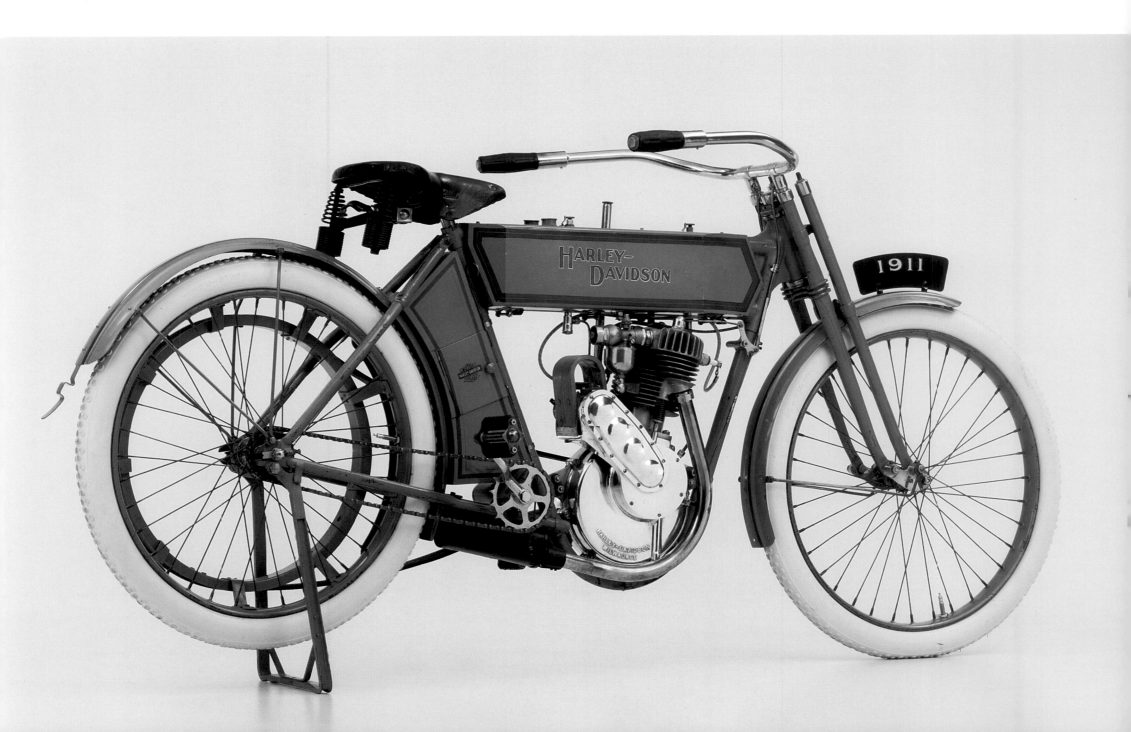

1912 Model X-8-A

———

"Our claims that the Harley-Davidson is the cleanest, most silent, most comfortable, and the most economical motorcycle made, are rather broad, but can easily be verified. Its extreme cleanliness is due to the fact that all moving parts requiring oil are enclosed. As for silence, the Harley-Davidson is known everywhere as the 'Silent Gray Fellow.'"

—Harley-Davidson dealer bulletin

In the summer of 2004, Archives staff cleaned this motorcycle and installed a new drive belt. In the process of their examinations, staff members discovered that this machine has several engineering prototype features and experimental changes. Some components appeared to be handmade. The freewheel pivot was welded onto the frame, which had an extension welded onto it. In addition, this vehicle has an experimental rear hub actuator, perhaps as a prototype or update for the freewheel mechanisms introduced in two-speed hubs in 1914.

For 1912, the company introduced a new frame that enhanced riding comfort through an innovation it called the "Ful-Floteing Seat." This invention put some of the helical coil springs from the cushion front fork into the seat tube to provide additional compliance to the Troxel seat. The Motor Company manufactured 545 belt-drive motorcycles in 1912, selling them for $235 apiece when equipped as this example.

1912 Model 8-X-E

"In laying out this year's work we planned ahead, as we usually do, and here is the way we planned: We would run the factory on single cylinder machines to its full capacity until we had a nice stock ahead of completed machines in crates, and also a big supply ready for assembling. Then we would take the smallest twin cylinder department and transfer some of our best mechanics out of the single cylinder department into the twin cylinder department, as it is easier to get machinists capable of working on single cylinders than on twins, especially regarding the timing of the valves, the timing of the magneto, etc. The plan also was to come out strong with the twin cylinders in June which would be right about in the middle of the good season.

"We did not advertise the twin cylinder at all, practically made no mention of it. The only places it was mentioned were where the trade papers were printing specifications. We had figured on coming out with a 'big noise' about June.

"The demand for this chain drive twin cylinder, however, is beyond anybody's expectations, even our Mr. Harley's who is very proud of this machine."

—Harley-Davidson dealer bulletin

This survivor represents the Motor Company's top-of-the-line offering for 1912. This 61-cubic-inch V-twin-powered model, which made its debut in the 1911 model year, used mechanically operated intake valves to solve the problems engineers experienced with the atmospheric valves powering earlier V-twin models.

The $285 V-twin model proved immensely popular, and the factory found it couldn't keep up with demand. Arthur Davidson addressed the situation in the announcement quoted above, which was sent to dealers and customers.

The announcement went on to warn dealers that demand had pushed delivery back 30 to 50 days, "And while we would like to be able to ship all the chain drive twin cylinders the dealers could use, I advise you candidly that we are not going to slight the machine or lower the standard in any way to rush deliveries."

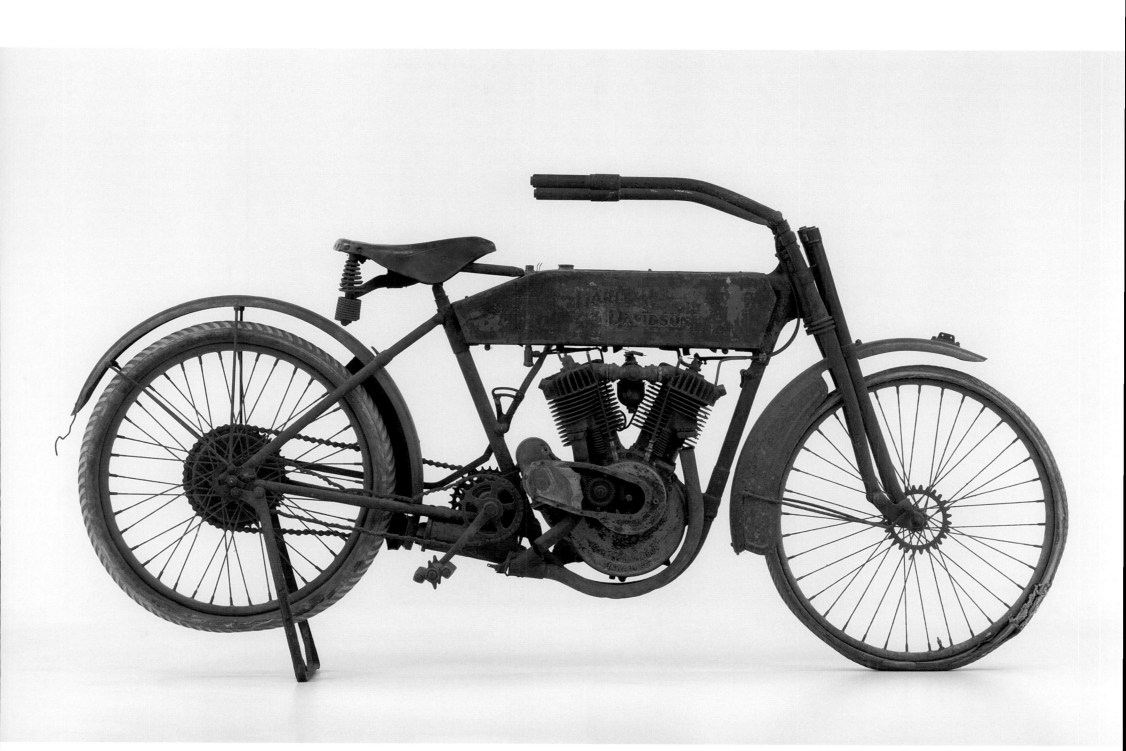

1913 Model 9-E

"Speed: In the Bakersfield, California, road race, Frank Lightner's stock Harley-Davidson (the kind you can buy, not a special racing machine) attained a speed of 68 miles an hour.

"Economy: The Harley-Davidson holds the World's Official Record for economy.

"Comfort: The Harley-Davidson is the only motorcycle which incorporates the Ful-Floteing Seat and Free Wheel Control. The Ful-Floteing Seat places 14 inches of concealed compressed springs between the rider and the bumps. The Free Wheel Control permits the starting and stopping of the machine without the tiresome pedaling or running alongside common with the ordinary motorcycles."

—Harley-Davidson advertisement

The year 1913 marked the third year of production for the twin, and Harley-Davidson introduced further engineering advances. Engineering rated engine output at 6.5 horsepower for 1911, improved output to "7 to 8 horsepower" for 1912, and bumped it to a solid 8 in 1913.

The Motor Company manufactured 6,732 of the $350 Model 9-E twins in 1913.

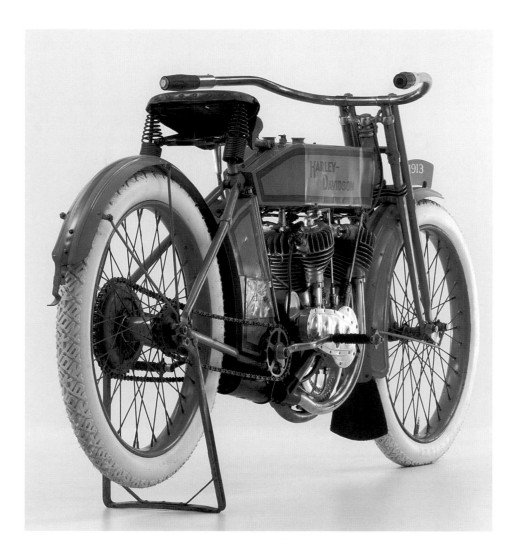

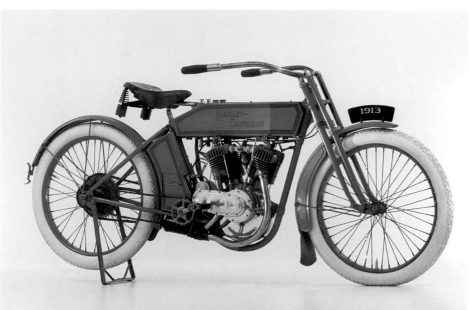

HARLEY-DAVIDSON

1914 Model 10-F

"The Harley-Davidson Band Brake, which is found only on the 1914 Harley-Davidson, is the most powerful brake on any motorcycle.

"It's the largest-braking surface, 7 5/16 inches in diameter, with 7/8 inch face. The axle is 5/8 inch.

"It's the simplest—has no small parts to break—nothing to get out of order. All working parts enclosed.

"The Harley-Davidson brake, like all other important parts of the 1914 Harley-Davidson, is manufactured and guaranteed by the Harley-Davidson Motor Company."

—Harley-Davidson advertisement

Model year 1914 saw the introduction of the Step-Starter. This enabled riders to start the engine on or off the centerstand, and it incorporated protection so that if the engine backfired, the mechanism would not kick back.

Harley-Davidson's manufacturing plant was now large enough and versatile enough to produce its own front and rear wheel hubs and rear band brakes.

The top-of-the-line Model 10-F came complete with rear luggage carrier and rectangular folding footboards. The company produced 7,956 of these $285 motorcycles.

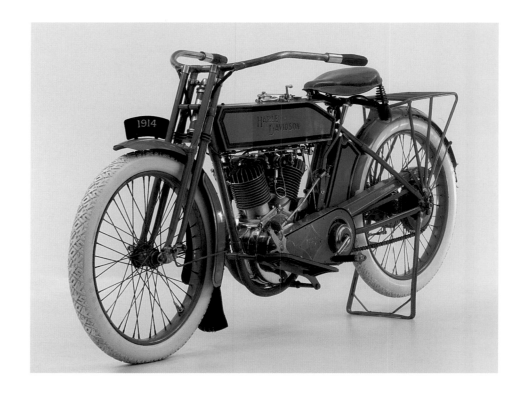

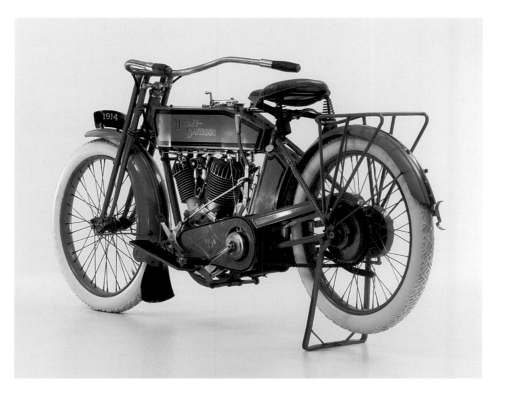

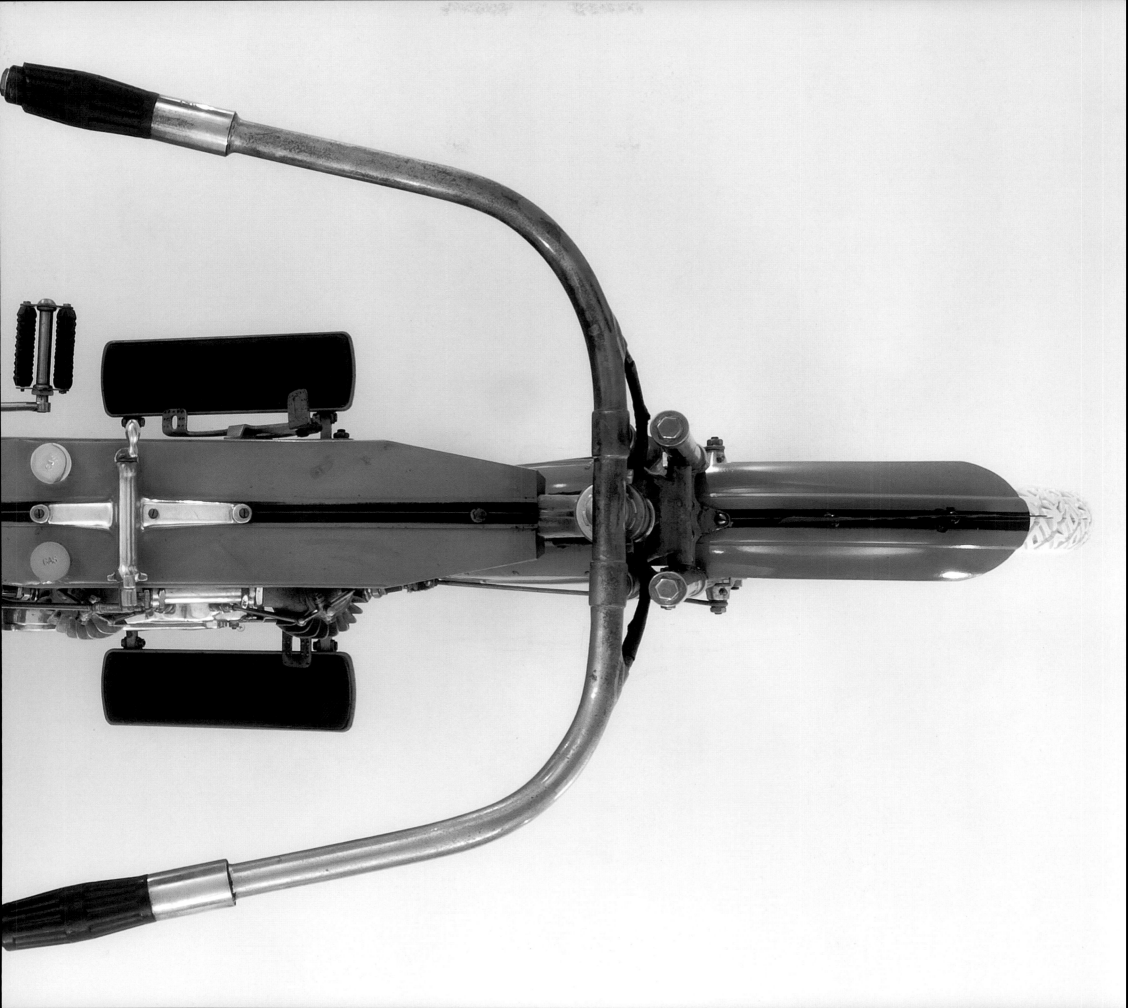

2
"Motorcycling—Outdoors' Greatest Sport"

F-Heads and Sport Twins: 1915–1928

War defined the world in which Harley-Davidson conducted business during its second decade, and not just war in Europe, but also along America's southern border. Brigadier General John Pershing took 4,000 men—on foot, on horseback, in trucks, and on motorcycles—into Mexico to pursue Pancho Villa, who had attacked ranches in Texas and New Mexico, killing 17 Americans.

For recreation, Americans watched motorcycles race at specially constructed board tracks and on dirt ovals normally used for horseracing. Motorcycling was increasingly seen as a recreational activity. Ford Motor Company cut the price of its Model T to $250 in August 1916, making four wheels cheaper than two.

This was a period of tremendous growth for the Harley-Davidson Motor Company. By the end of 1920, Harley-Davidson manufacturing facilities covered more than 400,000 square feet of space. Some 1,900 employees produced more than 24,000 motorcycles that year, and future opportunities appeared limitless. The "roar" heard during the Roaring Twenties often had the sound of a powerful V-twin motorcycle engine.

1915 Model 11-J

Electronics played an increasingly important role in motorcycle technology by 1915, and the H and J models of the 1915 Model 11 series could be equipped with Harley-Davidson's first complete electrical equipment kit. This package included a generator, headlight, taillight, and horn.

Engineering introduced several other improvements as well, such as new cylinders, larger fuel inlet ports, intake valves set in 45-degree seats, a larger intake manifold, and heavier flywheels. An automatic oiler improved lubrication, and an integral hand pump backed up automatic efforts. Engineering also added adjustable exhaust valves and more rigid connecting rods. The revised valve train on the F-head, 60.34-cubic-inch twin required Motor Company engineers to cut notches into the right side of the fuel tank on the bottom to accommodate the valves. A new, all-steel muffler reduced back pressure. All these updates, upgrades, and improvements increased power output by more than a third, from 8 horsepower up to 11.

The company assembled 3,719 Model J twins, selling them at $310.

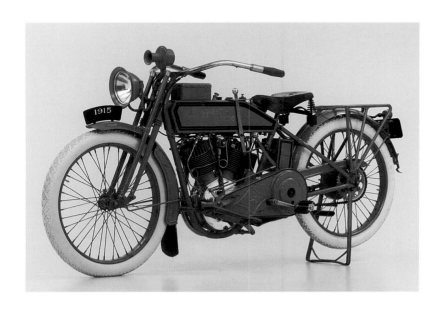

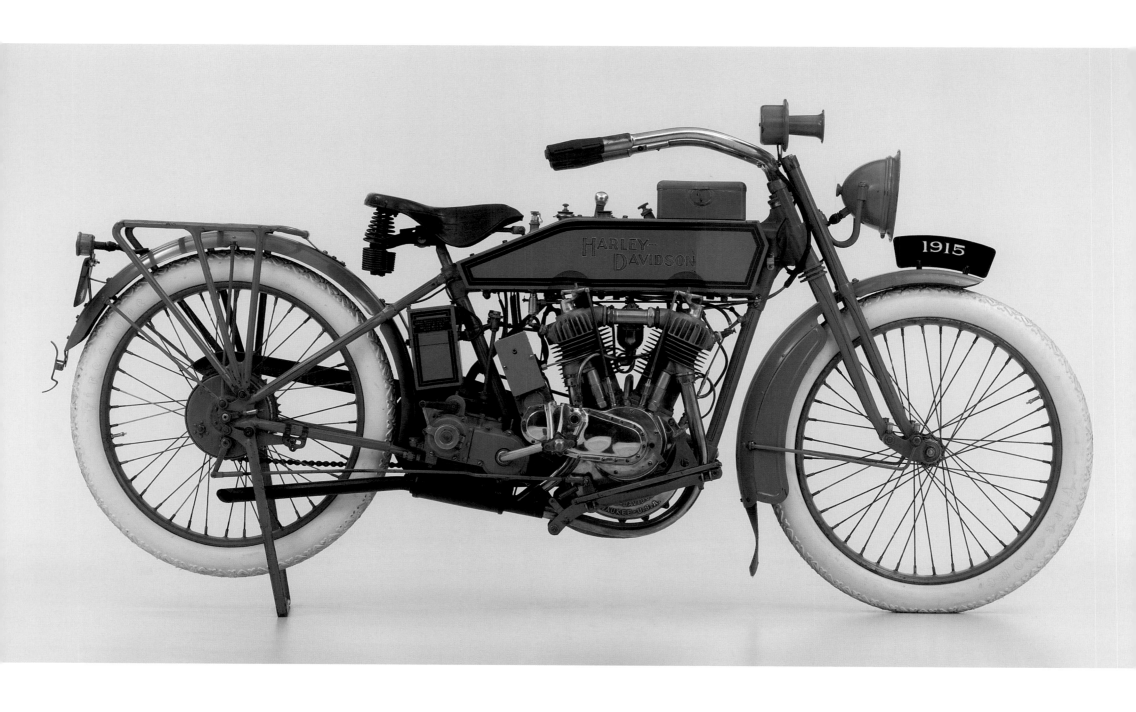

1916 Model 16-J with Model 16-M U.S. Postal Service Sidevan

Beginning with the 1916 model year, Harley-Davidson coordinated model numbers to match the year of production. Engineering, which handled the duties of styling appearance in those days, reshaped the fuel tank for 1916, giving it a sleeker, more rounded shape.

This 1916 Model 16-J has the bottom of its primary cover cut out, and it has no magneto, generator internals, or timing gears in the cam covers. It wears several coats of different paint and at one time was olive green, including the engine cases.

In 2005, Archives staff mounted an original, unrestored United States Postal Service package truck onto the motorcycle. The company manufactured 5,898 of the Model Js in 1916, selling them at $295. The 16-M Sidevan went for another $65.

1918 Model 18-J with Rogers Sidecar

The 1917 and 1918 models brought a significant color change to Harley-Davidson: the introduction of the color known as "Military Drab" (sometimes called Olive Drab). Harley-Davidson went one step further in late 1917 and through 1918 by painting the cases in the same color, as on this 1918 Model 18-J. Company literature extolled the virtues of the new color: "This makes the new Harley-Davidson the most beautiful machine which has ever left the Harley-Davidson factories. It is really a strange coincidence that within recent years various governments of the world have selected this color as the most serviceable for government equipment such as motorcycles, automobiles, and motor trucks."

After thoroughly cleaning this machine in 1999, Archives fitted it with a restored, single-passenger Rogers sidecar. The company manufactured 6,571 Model J motorcycles for 1918, selling them at $320 plus another $80 for the Rogers sidecar.

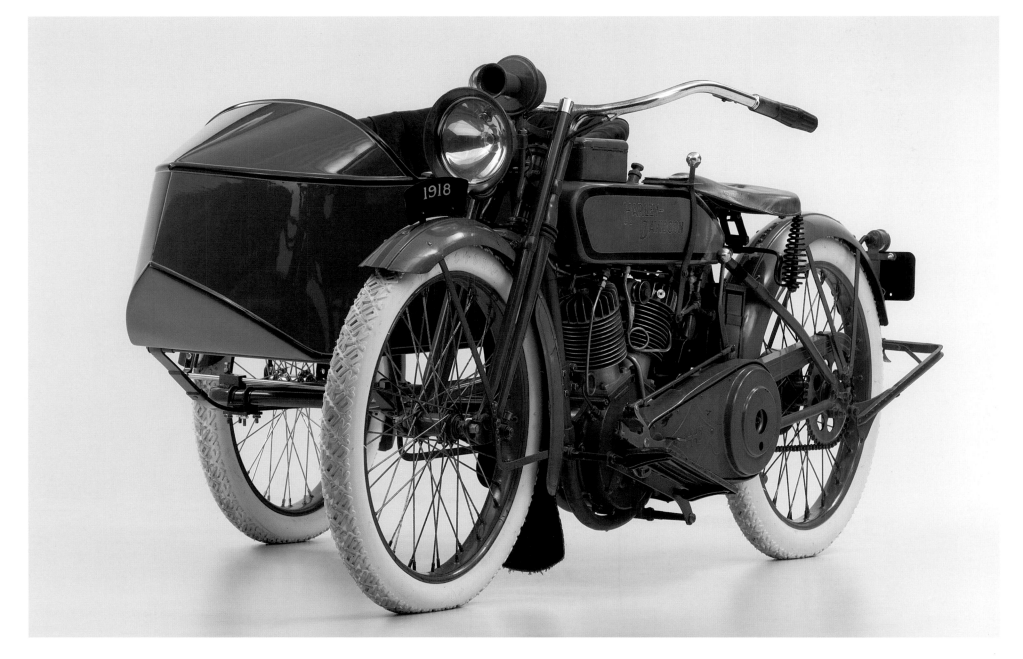

1919 Model 19-FUS Army

"War is the great test. Only the trustworthy—the strong—the efficient—survive. The Harley-Davidson put to the test 'over there' emerged a striking example of the survival of the fittest—proven under fire.

"Fleeting out over the scarred and broken road-beds and across shell-torn battlefields, as the flying squadron gets into action—facing the zip, snap and crackle of machine guns—carrying the officer or dispatch rider on his mission of peril, or bringing one more machine gun 'closer up'—the Harley-Davidson proudly shoulders an ever-increasing responsibility of service—and gets there. Sturdy, mobile, surprisingly economical, in the service of the Allies long before America entered the conflict, it weathered the grueling demands of war, and the severe criticisms of military experts.

"From the very beginning the Harley-Davidson has been built to stand up under extraordinary service. When it was put to the one supreme test it made good."

—Harley-Davidson advertisement

The company manufactured 7,521 of the Model 19-FUS Army for the U.S. government in 1919. The civilian Model 19-F sold for $350. Harley-Davidson sold the motorcycle to the government for considerably less. Military versions have flatter front fenders to better resist mud packing between the tire and fender. Civilian versions received Brewster Green striping on the toolbox and tank, a decorative treatment the army deleted from its motorcycles.

1919 Model 19-J and 1920 Model 20-J

The role of vehicle preservation has changed over the years. At one time, preservation meant full restoration. The goal of vehicle archivists at Harley-Davidson has been preventing further deterioration. The two motorcycles shown here, the unrestored, original "time capsule" 1919 Model 19-J on the left and the preserved and cleaned 1920 Model 20-J on the right, provide examples of that philosophy.

Both motorcycles have the full electrical package, including the headlight, taillight, horn, and generator. The company manufactured 9,941 examples of the Model 19-J, selling them for $370 apiece. The preserved and cleaned 1920 model's saddle is a Messinger Air-Cushion, a $1.50 option in 1920, but standard equipment in 1921. This example does not have a serial number, though it is equipped with regular production parts. Harley-Davidson sold the Model 20-J for $395 and assembled 14,192 of them in 1920.

1920 Model 20-W Sport

"The Woman's Outdoor Companion. . . . It is the feature-refined woman-kind. . . . Motorcycling among women has become accepted as much as horseback riding in days gone by, and the Harley-Davidson responds to the guiding hand of woman as did the kindest tempered steed of old. If you're an out-door girl or woman, you'll glory in the 'git' and the 'go' of motorcycling."

—Harley-Davidson advertisement

The Model 20-W Sport, developed primarily for the export market, is truly unique among all Harley-Davidson motorcycles, with its fore-and-aft-mounted, opposed twin-cylinder engine set in a Keystone-type frame that utilizes the engine as a stress-bearing member. The engine displaces 35.6 cubic inches, or 584 cubic centimeters. The company introduced the machine in 1919, and sales grew slowly. The W Sport employs a trailing link front suspension attached to tubes containing helical coil springs, a configuration not seen before or after the W Sport models. The W weighs roughly 257 pounds. The engine of this particular example is partially cut away, possibly for marketing or display purposes to show the many differences between the traditional V-twins and this horizontally opposed engine. The company manufactured 4,459 W Sports in 1920 and sold them for $335.

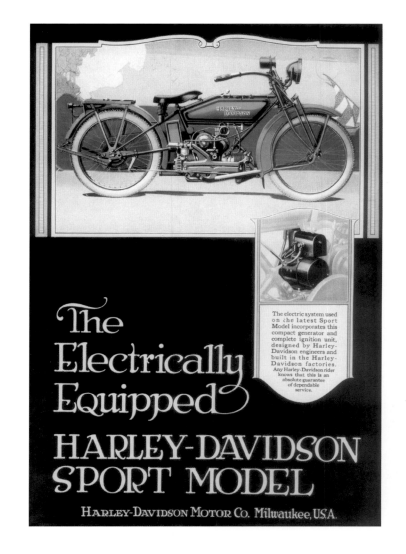

The electric system used on the latest Sport Model incorporates this compact generator and complete ignition unit, designed by Harley-Davidson engineers and built in the Harley-Davidson factories. Any Harley-Davidson rider knows that this is an absolute guarantee of dependable service.

The
Electrically
Equipped
HARLEY-DAVIDSON
SPORT MODEL

HARLEY-DAVIDSON MOTOR CO. Milwaukee, U.S.A.

1923 Model JDCA

Harley-Davidson introduced the Model JDCA for 1921. The new engine, with 74 cubic inches of displacement, had a bore and stroke of 3.4375x4 inches and developed 18 horsepower. Aluminum pistons kept weight down and helped the motor to rev more quickly, leading to its internal nickname, the "Fast Stock" motor. Company advertising referred to it as the "Superpowered Twin" and emphasized that the new "74" was designed for tandem and sidecar riding, while the steadfast "61s" remained the choice for solo riders. On this particular example, a $5 option got the purchaser a toolbox top–mounted Weston ammeter and a gas tank top–mounted Corbin 80-miles-per-hour speedometer.

Starting in 1922, Harley-Davidson painted its motorcycles Brewster Green, an extremely dark variation that, with age, appears almost black. Olive Drab still was offered as an option. An innovative hinged rear fender appeared in 1923 to facilitate rear wheel removal for easier tire changes.

The Motor Company manufactured 7,458 of the Model JD vehicles (the breakdown for CA versions is unknown). The JD sold for $330, and the CA options cost an additional $10.

1925 Model FE with 1928 Model QT Left-Hand Two-Passenger Tourist Sidecar

The 1928 Model QT sidecar rig with its left-hand mount was sold primarily into foreign markets. The car allows two passengers to sit side by side. It has leaf springs in the front and one-quarter elliptical springs under the rear. Archives records indicate this likely is a reproduction sidecar.

In 1999, Archives acquired this 1925 Model FE sidecar rig, fully restored except for the sidecar tub and upholstery. A few details remain incorrect. The tank stripe pattern is from the 1926-and-later models instead of 1925, and the

cylinders should be nickel plated instead of painted silver.

The motorcycle used iron-alloy pistons in place of the less-successful aluminum pistons introduced in 1923. Harley-Davidson's color scheme had returned to Olive Drab green for 1924, and that color (combined with maroon striping) continued through 1925. The company assembled 1,318 of the FE models for the 1925 model year. This model sold for $295, and the two-seat sidecar cost another $130.

1925 Model JDCB

"Speed in every line—strength in every curve—low hung for safety and bigger-tired for luxurious comfort. . . . Newest and finest model of the World's Greatest Motorcycle—the 1925 'Stream-Line' Harley-Davidson. How the young bloods will itch to get this handsome, speedy, peppy, thoroughbred out for a spin."

—Harley-Davidson advertisement

While the styling of the 1925 Model JDCB satisfied the needs of speed-crazed customers, the model experienced technical problems. The aluminum-alloy pistons of 1923 failed to meet the company's expectations, and engineers quickly changed to a new iron alloy for piston castings. The company manufactured 9,506 JDCB models. It sold the motorcycles for $335.

The 1925 HARLEY-DAVIDSON
with 27 Big Improvements

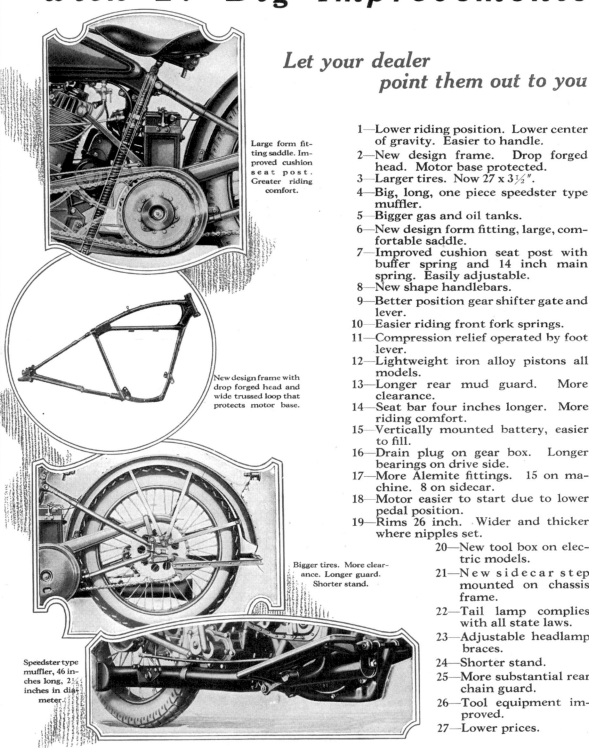

Let your dealer
point them out to you

Large form fitting saddle. Improved cushion seat post. Greater riding comfort.

New design frame with drop forged head and wide trussed loop that protects motor base.

Bigger tires. More clearance. Longer guard. Shorter stand.

Speedster type muffler, 46 inches long, 2¼ inches in diameter.

1—Lower riding position. Lower center of gravity. Easier to handle.
2—New design frame. Drop forged head. Motor base protected.
3—Larger tires. Now 27 x 3½".
4—Big, long, one piece speedster type muffler.
5—Bigger gas and oil tanks.
6—New design form fitting, large, comfortable saddle.
7—Improved cushion seat post with buffer spring and 14 inch main spring. Easily adjustable.
8—New shape handlebars.
9—Better position gear shifter gate and lever.
10—Easier riding front fork springs.
11—Compression relief operated by foot lever.
12—Lightweight iron alloy pistons all models.
13—Longer rear mud guard. More clearance.
14—Seat bar four inches longer. More riding comfort.
15—Vertically mounted battery, easier to fill.
16—Drain plug on gear box. Longer bearings on drive side.
17—More Alemite fittings. 15 on machine. 8 on sidecar.
18—Motor easier to start due to lower pedal position.
19—Rims 26 inch. Wider and thicker where nipples set.
20—New tool box on electric models.
21—New sidecar step mounted on chassis frame.
22—Tail lamp complies with all state laws.
23—Adjustable headlamp braces.
24—Shorter stand.
25—More substantial rear chain guard.
26—Tool equipment improved.
27—Lower prices.

1930s Mead Ice Yacht "Whirlwind" Model

Mead Gliders of Chicago, Illinois, sold plans, unassembled kits, and complete and running motorized ice boats. The builder of this example used a 1925 JDCB 74-inch twin engine with magneto ignition installed instead of a generator. The motorcycle engine drives a pulley connected to a 4-foot propeller. The "boat" hull was fabricated out of bent spruce covered with canvas and painted. It has a dual-seat cockpit, which accommodates a driver and passenger in tandem. Driver controls consist only of a steering wheel, brake lever (which simply jams a length of wood into the ice), throttle, and kill switch. Archives records indicate that the original purchaser in February 1940 lived in Elizabeth, New Jersey. Mead sold the complete kit, ready to assemble, for $49.50, while the finished Ice Yacht, assembled in Chicago and shipped ready for the purchaser to install an engine, went for $149.50 plus an additional $10 for crating. Blueprints alone sold for $2.00.

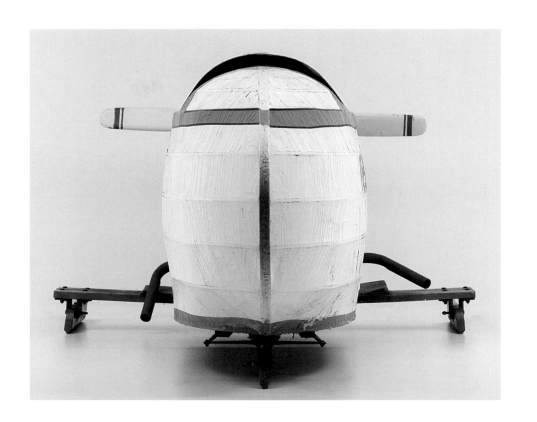

1928 Model JH

Called the "Two-Cam Sixty-One," the 1928 Model JH introduced a new engine line to the Harley-Davidson enthusiast. Inside the engine, two camshafts operated intake and exhaust valves, and the Dow metal pistons were domed in order to produce a higher compression ratio. In 1928, Harley-Davidson introduced front wheel brakes and an air cleaner on the Model JH. This example is painted Police Blue, one of four optional colors in addition to the standard Olive Drab green (though buyers could order nearly any color if they were willing to pay extra). Red-and-gold striping cost an extra $7.

This example has both front and rear stands and is equipped with the 46-inch-long Speedster-type muffler with a foot-operated cut-out. Harley-Davidson did not include the JH on its 1928 price lists, but Archives information indicates it sold for $320. The factory manufactured a total of 4,184 Model J motorcycles, but the breakdown for JH models is not available.

3

"Gee, Dad! Buy me a Harley-Davidson."

The Bicycles: 1917–1923

The bicycling craze that led to the development of motorcycles resurged in the late 1910s and gathered momentum in the early 1920s. Harley-Davidson offered a full line of men's, women's, and children's bikes during this period, and the company promoted them heavily.

"Most All the Fellows have Harley-Davidsons, Dad," read the headline on an advertisement from 1919. "Wherever 'the bunch' gets together, you'll find most of the fellows ride the classy-looking, easy-running Harley-Davidson—'America's Finest Bicycle.'"

Another holiday-season promotion called it "The Gift of His Dreams—a Harley-Davidson Bicycle." The copy went on to remind fathers that "every boy dreams of the day when he'll have a new bike just as he dreams of the day he'll be a man. Didn't you dream those dreams when you were a boy?"

1917 Model 5-17 Boy Scout Bicycle and 1920 Model 420 Motorcyke Tank Bicycle

In 1917, a father could give his son the Harley-Davidson dream for just $30. The company named its Model 5-17 the "Boy Scout." This title lasted only one year, and Archives staff suspect the Boy Scouts of America objected to commercializing their name, forcing the Motor Company to rename the model. The company offered this bicycle on special 20-inch tires mounted on 28-spoke wooden rims. It also had a New Departure brake mechanism.

Harley-Davidson introduced the Motorcyke in order to fill dealer and customer demand for a bicycle that more closely resembled a motorcycle. The company contracted with Davis Sewing Machine Company of Watertown, New York, and Dayton, Ohio, to manufacture the bicycles. Davis created a motorcycle-style double-truss frame with a trussed front fork. The braced Shelby handlebars are equipped with bulldog-style wooden grips. The dealer who delivered this bicycle fitted it with an accessory headlight with batteries concealed inside the in-frame tank, which is decorated with the Harley-Davidson name on the side. With its plunger-type horn and accessory luggage rack, it looks the part. It sold for $56 in 1920.

1918 Model 3-18 Ladies' Standard Bicycle and 1919 Model 9-19 Gentlemen's Roadster Bicycle

The Ladies' Standard model was Harley-Davidson's deluxe women's bicycle during this period. It featured a full chain guard that surrounded the 26-tooth front chain ring with the patented repeating H-D logo design. It had a waterproof Troxel seat, and the rear fender was fitted with the string "skirt guard."

Harley-Davidson offered this Gentlemen's Roadster only in 1918 and 1919. The Roadster was the company's sporting men's bicycle, and it used the racing frame with outside brazed joints, the racing front fork, and the same wooden handgrips wrapped in leather as appeared on the company's Racer model. This example does include fenders, along with the H-D logo front chain ring. In 1918, Harley-Davidson sold the Gentlemen's Roadster for $46 and the Ladies' Standard for $40.

1918 Model 8-18 "The Racer" Bicycle

Competition had become part of Harley-Davidson's DNA by the time the Model 8-18 bicycle appeared in 1918. Board-track bicycle races at the turn of the century gave rise to board-track motorcycle and automobile races a decade later, and the evolutionary cycle came full circle by the late 1910s. Track racers were bicycles in the purest form: no brakes, headlights, batteries, tanks, or fenders. Nothing was allowed that added weight.

Davis Sewing Machine Company in Dayton, Ohio, manufactured the parts and other bicycles for Harley-Davidson. Davis produced these racers with Torrington racing pedals fitted with toe clips. The company used full-nickel racing front forks, a special nickel-steel "Hans Renold" bush roller block racing chain, Lawson racing handlebars, "knock-off" rear-axle nuts, and racing saddle. William Harley patented the repeating-logo H-D front chain ring. With its fragile-looking, 36-spoke, wooden-rim racing wheels and slender tires, and with neither coaster nor hand brakes and no coasting freewheel, the Racer weighed just 22 pounds and sold new for $45.

This model is equipped with Firestone non-skid black tread red side wall motorcycle fabric tires

And Now—A Harley-Davidson Bicycle

Beauty—of line and finish—dependability, balance and quality —all the experience-bought knowledge gained in more than fifteen years of high-grade motorcycle building, characterize the Harley-Davidson line of bicycles for men and women, boys and girls. There are seven distinctive models. The

Harley-Davidson Bicycle

is a wheel you will be proud to ride. Like the motorcycle, it is finished in a beautiful military olive drab. It has finely adjusted steering head bearings, which with specially designed front forks provide unsurpassed light steering qualities.

Sturdy, balanced hangers and carefully ground bearings insure easy running. Rims, spokes, hubs, coaster brakes, saddles and tires are all of the same high quality that has helped the Harley-Davidson motorcycle to smash speed and endurance records year after year. And this bicycle is not high priced. Tremendous production enables us to sell Harley-Davidson bicycles at prices you might expect to pay for wheels possessing less merit. Don't be satisfied with any bicycle but a Harley-Davidson. See one at your dealers—write for descriptive literature.

HARLEY-DAVIDSON MOTOR COMPANY

Producers of High-Grade Motorcycles for More Than Fifteen Years
481 B Street, MILWAUKEE, WIS., U. S. A.

4

"Ride a Winner"

Early Race Machines: 1916–1935

Racing, whether on motorcycles, bicycles, or in automobiles, proved the best escape from the depressing news coming from Europe as World War I spread across the continent. Harley-Davidson's racing motorcycles competed and won at racetracks across the country (and around the world), building demand for the company's motorcycles both in the United States and abroad. Racing remained a popular distraction even into the Great Depression, by which time Harley's machines had become as dominant a force in motorcycle racing as the company's production bikes were in the motorcycle market.

1916 Model T Factory Racer

In 1914, William "Bill" Ottaway, William Harley's assistant chief engineer and the company competition director, designed an all-out competition engine for the Motor Company. For several years prior, Harley-Davidson and numerous privateers campaigned modified production engines and achieved some success. The idea of a higher-horsepower, higher-revving, strictly competition engine was a dream of both privateers and factory riders.

Ottaway created the engine for what became the Model T by fitting a special camshaft that held intake and exhaust valves open longer and higher. He then polished and further enlarged the intake and exhaust ports. No one now really knows how much horsepower these engines developed, but they were potent enough that riders encountered serious handling problems at very high speeds. Ottaway worked to adjust the fork links and tube lengths to subdue the wobble.

This complete correct example is the only Model T with Ottaway's engine known to exist. His race frame utilizes a front fork that is 1 inch shorter than standard production models, and it includes a special mechanism to compress the springs.

1920 Model FCA "Banjo-Case" Two-Cam Racer

In early 1919, William Ottaway hired a stable of riders, including Ray Weishaar, Jim Davis, Otto Walker, Ralph Hepburn, Fred Ludlow, Leslie "Red" Parkhurst, and Walter Higley. Officially they were called Harley-Davidson team riders, but they soon became known as the "Wrecking Crew" for their total domination of racing events. Each of these skilled riders had an effective machine under him, and each had a near perfectionist—Ottaway—as his manager. He drilled riders and mechanics on pit-stop techniques; he was among the first racing managers to recognize that if riders and machines were virtually equal, teams could win or lose the race because of time wasted in the pits.

For 1919, Ottaway had a new tool: the "Banjo-Case" Model FCA Two-Cam, a 60.34-cubic-inch "pocket valve" V-twin. The Banjo Two-Cam won so many races that newspaper headline writers ran out of ways to describe the victories. The engines were special. "These motors are not production motors," a typed bulletin from Ottaway's competition department advised. "The entire crank case and cam action is made by hand. Only flywheels, connecting rods, shafts, pistons, and cylinders are regular FCA parts and can be supplied from manufacturing stock. These parts, however, are not the same as our present production models. When ordering parts, it is absolutely necessary to give the motor number, and if the name is uncertain or not sufficiently descriptive, a sketch or photograph of what is wanted will be of assistance and save annoying delays."

This motorcycle, which carries motor number CA12, is the only complete and virtually original example known to exist. It has its original race engine, forks, gas tank, spark plugs, and frame. Some documents suggest Harley-Davidson set a price of $1,400 for each of these motorcycles, high enough to dissuade privateers from buying them.

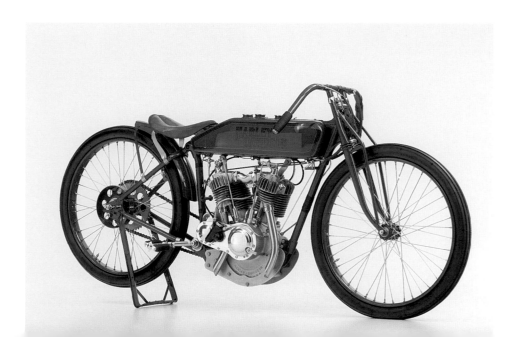

1923 "Banjo-Case" 8-Valve Racer

This is one of only two remaining examples of the 1923 "Banjo-Case" 8-Valve Racer with an original banjo-case race engine. The term *banjo case* refers to the resemblance the primary gear cover has to the musical instrument carrying case. Englishman Fred Dixon originally raced this particular motorcycle. Following his death, Seattle, Washington, dealer Marion Diedericks acquired the bike from Dixon's estate. Boozefighters Motorcycle Club member John Cameron later purchased it from Diedericks. Cameron modified and raced the engine.

The motorcycle shown here has the original racing handlebar, fork, and gas tank (although records suggest one side may have been rebuilt). The scissor shock absorber on the front fork also is original. A number of Harley-Davidson riders rode these 8-valve racers to victories at average speeds greater than 100 miles per hour.

It is uncertain how many banjo-case 8-valve racers were produced. The Motor Company priced them at $1,500, about four times the cost of their competitors' 8-valve motorcycles.

Otto Walker on Harley-Davidson eight valve machine which averaged 104.43 m.p.h. in 25 mile race at Beverly, California, April 24, 1921

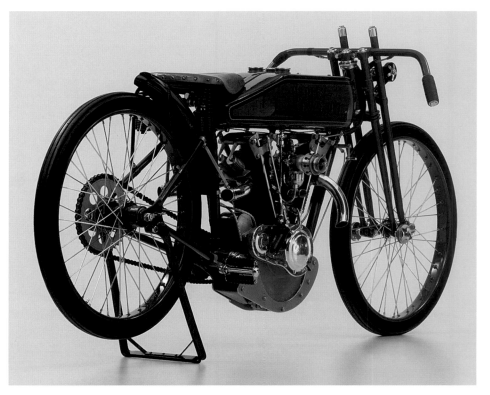

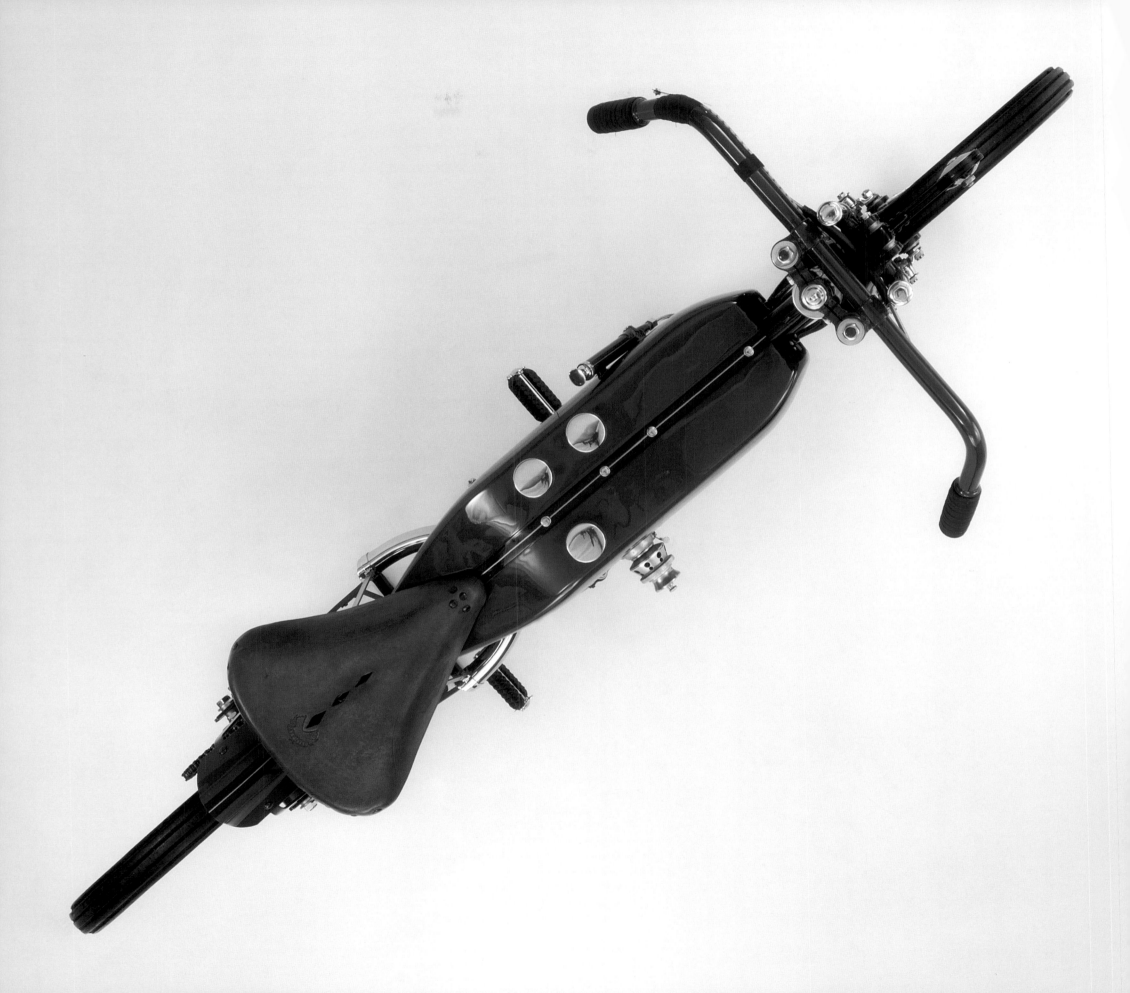

1924 Model FH "Indirect Action" Two-Cam Racer

Harley-Davidson produced "indirect action" twin-cam engines only during 1923 and 1924. The Model FH Two-Cam Racer shown here is the only one known to have survived intact. The engine dominated professional racing across the United States, competing in both dirt-track and board-track events.

Engines of this design lack the removable tappet blocks visible in the later "direct action" design. Instead they incorporate cam followers actuating lifter pins.

This racer's frame was an original board-track racing version and, as configured, included racing front and rear forks, a racing handlebar, a fuel tank, and an uncommon rear friction/compensating hub. This original engine still has its racing spark plugs and the straight-fin Harry Ricardo–designed cylinders. Racer Red Davis set up and competed on this particular motorcycle.

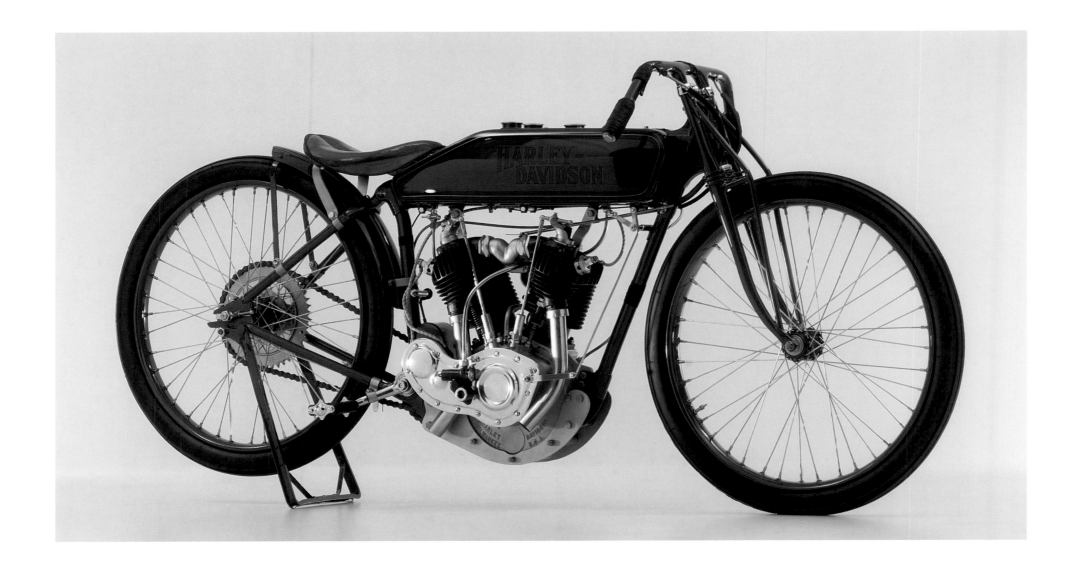

1924 FHAC Two-Cam Road Racer

The FHAC designation applied to special 60.34-cubic-inch, 1,000cc two-cam engines in "lowboy keystone" frames that Harley-Davidson devised for road racing and hillclimb events. The Motor Company used these only through 1925. The lower profile of this frame required deep semicircular notches in the fuel tank to accommodate the intake valve gear.

Claude Ceresole of Berne, Switzerland, owned and raced this particular motorcycle. There is some evidence that he received factory support. Ceresole won the Swiss 1,000cc championships in 1924, 1925, 1927, and 1929 on this motorcycle.

Ceresole's racer has no front fender and a cut-back rear fender. His turned-down handlebars have taped grips. He left exposed both the primary and secondary chains, presumably for faster replacement should one fail during a race. He also welded extra support tubing to the front fork legs for additional strength. This motorcycle is in preserved original condition.

1926 Model FHAC "Direct Action" Two-Cam Racer

The term "direct action" refers to a system in which tappet block plates bolt directly to the crankcase. Indirect action, the earlier system, meant these tappet blocks (or the housings surrounding and supporting the tappets) were a seamless part, set into the crankcase casting. This example had tapered cylinder fins that Harry Ricardo designed and patented following his work with the Motor Company. The short-coupled frame is a reproduction, and records suggest the handlebar may be as well. The forks are 1915-style, which, according to Archives information, is correct for this model. The wide racing gas tanks are original.

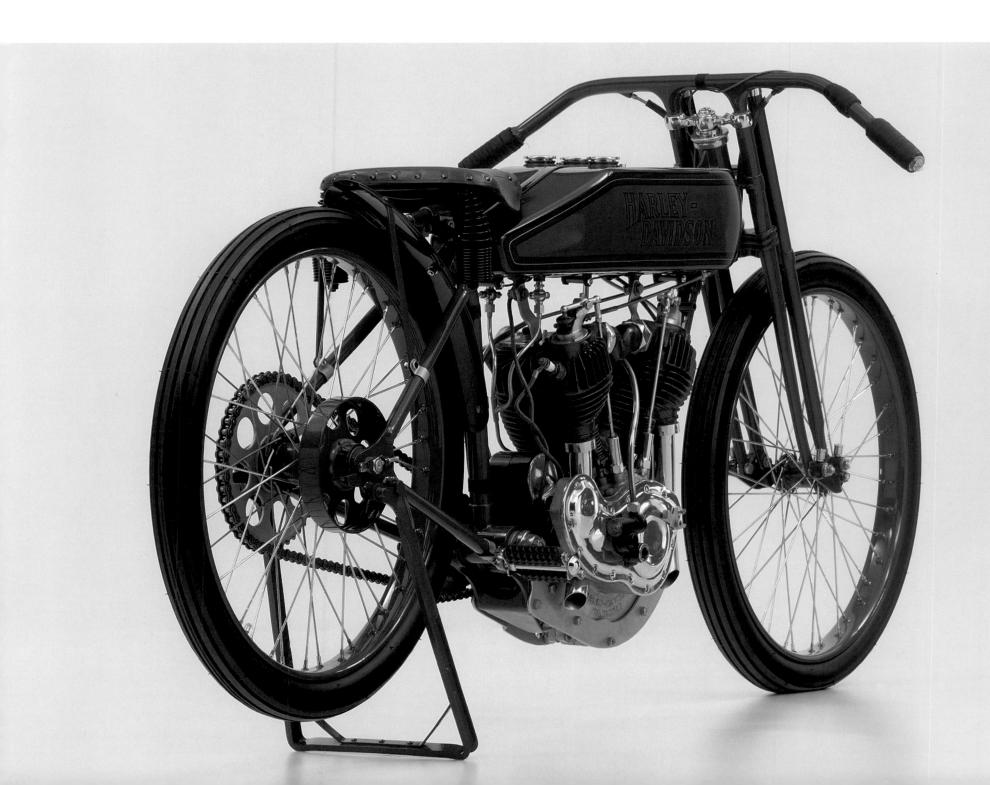

1930 Model BAH Hillclimber

The 1930 Model BAH Hillclimber used a 500cc, overhead-valve single engine, but inspection suggests the cylinder on this example is not a Harley-Davidson barrel. One of this motorcycle's owners/competitors extensively modified the frame to accommodate a smaller homemade gas tank and to add grab bars for hillclimbing.

Restorers had to fabricate a replacement shift lever under the seat, exhaust pipes, carburetor flange, fuel and oil lines, crankcase breather, and clutch pedal. They also mounted a chain on the rear tire.

5
"More Thrills than Ever"

Early Flatheads: 1926–1941

The thriving 1920s economy continued in full bloom until it came to a shuddering halt on Black Thursday, October 24, 1929, when prices on the New York Stock Exchange collapsed. It would take another few years for the impact to reach businesses and citizens throughout the world, but when it hit, it would take all but the strongest companies down in a wave of economic chaos.

Like all businesses during this period, the Harley-Davidson Motor Company struggled to survive, yet throughout the Depression the company continued to produce innovative products of the highest quality.

The period that preceded World War II marked a time of innovation in motorcycle engine technology, one that saw side-valve design emerge as the predominant configuration. While we view flatheads as anachronistic today, given the quality of fuel and the metallurgy of the period, side-valve designs represented the state of the art in engine configurations in the 1930s.

1926 Model BA

In the early 1920s, Harley-Davidson looked to Japan and Europe as potential targets for increasing sales. The company marketed its compact 345cc (21.1-cubic-inch) B and BA models, the Single and Sporting Single, for individual transportation in those markets. These bikes used a new single-cylinder engine rated at around 12 horsepower. Standard models used a side-valve (flathead) design with iron-alloy pistons, while the sporting version, which was produced from 1926 until 1929, used overhead valves and aluminum pistons. Side-valve B models sold for $235, while the overhead-valve BA versions listed at $275.

Archives records report that the BA returned 70 to 80 miles per gallon. This motorcycle is painted in factory Olive Green. In 1926, Harley-Davidson manufactured only 515 Model BA motorcycles.

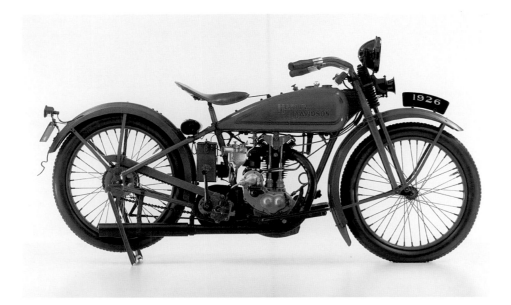

1929 Model C

"Here it is . . . Harley-Davidson's latest masterpiece, the New 500 c.c. Single. With its low, graceful lines, flashing speed, and thrilling acceleration, the New Single has captured the hearts of motorcyclists the world over. . . . As the latest addition to the world-renowned Harley-Davidson family, this new thoroughbred deserves your careful consideration."

—Harley-Davidson advertisement

The company added the new 500cc Model C line to its production of single-cylinder motors. To improve performance, engineering fitted Harry Ricardo's side-valve heads. A complex but effective new exhaust muffler system incorporated four tubes and provided dual-side exhaust for the single-cylinder engine. The carburetor was a Schebler Deluxe with a self-cleaning air filter.

Twin headlights sat above the gaping horn opening and gave the motorcycle a distinctive face. Model C bikes shared their frames with the D-series 45-cubic-inch twins. Harley-Davidson introduced the Model C late in the 1929 model year and produced just 1,570 of the new bikes, for sale at $255.

1929 Model DL

When Harley-Davidson developed its new 45-cubic-inch, side-valve engine for the 1929 model year, the large vertical generator was mounted off the left front corner of the crankcase casting. From a distance, this large shape resembles a third cylinder, and its silhouette made customers and competitors think the Motor Company had introduced a triple.

The company initially offered a low-compression version (Model D) of the new 45-cubic-inch twin in 1929, but engineering took advantage of Harry Ricardo's removable head design on the new DL models. The DL (and D) shared a frame and a 56.5-inch wheelbase with the 500cc Model C that the company introduced around the same time. In 1929, Harley-Davidson manufactured 2,343 of the Model DL, selling them for $290.

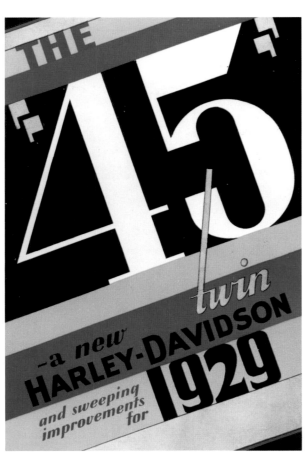

1930 Model VL with 1928 Model MC Package Truck

Harley-Davidson's replacement for the Model J appeared in late 1929, and the company designated it the VL. With Harry Ricardo–designed cylinders and removable heads, this model replaced the last of Harley-Davidson's DeDion-type intake-over-exhaust (F-head) engines, which the company had used since 1903. This 74-cubic-inch engine developed between 26 and 28 horsepower using magnesium pistons. Its flathead/side-valve configuration offered owners the convenience—and economy—of easily removable heads that allowed the valves to be ground and other maintenance to be performed without removing the entire engine from the frame.

Loaded with gasoline and oil, the VL weighed around 550 pounds. Engineering fitted an internally expanding rear drum brake, replacing the external contracting style previously in use. This was the last year for the unsuccessful twin headlights, which put out less light than the previous single-lamp design.

Archives staff cleaned this VL in 2002, at which time they installed the restored Package Truck on the motorcycle. It is painted dark blue and cream, while the package truck is black with gold striping and Gulf Oil logos. In 1930, the company produced 3,246 VLs, selling them for $340. The original price of the package truck is unknown.

1932 Model VLD

"Split the air like a rocket! Flashing acceleration—from start to full speed in a few seconds—is a motorcycle thrill that only a 'rocket motor' could equal. Just ride a 1932 Harley-Davidson and feel what real pick-up is. See how it shoots you away from tangled traffic. You are down the road, safe, and clear, before cars are really rolling. Then the whole countryside is yours—for swift jaunt or long tour. And motorcycling costs so little!"

—Harley-Davidson advertisement

While the wordsmiths in advertising and promotion crafted eloquent prose at one end of the large factory complex, the engineers improved on the VL models with new crankcases, cams, valve gear, frames, and constant mesh starters at the other end. The Motor Company produced 2,684 VL models in 1932 and sold them for $320 each.

1932 Model G Servi-Car

The year 1932 is generally regarded as the debut year of the Servi-Cars. The company powered these three-wheeled service vehicles with the 45-cubic-inch flathead engine and fitted them with three-speed transmissions. Archives records suggest that some of these utility machines may have appeared sometime in 1931 in local testing. The rear fenders mounted on the example here were unique to the first year. The G version did not have either a front tow bar, rear bumper, or speedometer among its standard equipment. First year sales figures and selling prices are unknown.

HARLEY-DAVIDSON

SERVI-CAR » » » » »

» » » » » THE MODERN METHOD FOR

PROFITABLE

PICK-UP AND DELIVERY
OF AUTOMOBILES ....

SAVES AN EXTRA MAN'S TIME.... — Servi-Car does away with the need for sending out two men and a car to pick up or deliver a customer's automobile. It saves the cost of one man's wages and doubles and trebles the profits on the other man's working time.

» » SAVES HIGH CAR EXPENSE.... — Cuts down the gas, oil, tire and depreciation cost of pick-up and delivery with a car. Prevents the losses occasioned through use of service or tow cars in this work, when that equipment can be used more profitably elsewhere.

» » ANYONE CAN OPERATE IT.... — Servi-Car can be driven by anyone in your present organization. Avoids the necessity of hiring inefficient transient drivers during rush periods. Permits sending out employees especially adept in handling certain customer contracts.

» » INCREASES SERVICE SALES.... — Convenient pick-up and delivery enables your service manager to sell many service jobs that might not come to you otherwise. Specials featured by telephone or advertising will be taken advantage of by many more customers.

» » EFFECTIVE ADVERTISING.... — Servi-Car's eye-catching appearance, plus the message that can be easily lettered on it, is one of the most effective advertising mediums you could employ. Every pick-up and delivery is an advertisement reaching a multitude of prospects.

A story in efficiency. One man goes out to pick up a customer's car, hooks Servi-Car to the bumper and drives the car back. Time saved, operating cost cut to the minimum, wages saved and profits gained on the job.

AUTO SERVICE

1933 Model VLD

The 1933 VLD "Special Sport Solo" was the new hot rod version of the VL series. Harley-Davidson gave this engine an efficient new Y-shaped intake manifold and lightweight magnesium-alloy pistons. Engineering installed new cylinder barrels and Harry Ricardo–style removable side-valve heads. These improvements boosted engine output to 36 horsepower, 20 percent more than the tamer VL series. Factory literature refers to this as the "T.N.T. Motor."

The company introduced two-tone paint as standard equipment, and this was the first Harley-Davidson model to have a full pan seat. An art deco eagle adorned the fuel tank. This example may have been pulled straight from production for the company's growing collection of historic motorcycles. While the engine cases appear unused, the cylinder barrels and heads appear well run, suggesting this also could have been an engineering development bike.

The company manufactured just 780 VLDs in 1933, selling them at $320, compared with the high-compression VL and the standard V, both of which cost $310. This color combination is Mandarin Red and black.

1933 Model VLD with
1934 Model LT Sidecar

This Special Sport Solo motorcycle model mated to a sidecar is an unusual—and heavily optioned—machine. It appears in an optional silver and turquoise paint and has a full array of optional lights, as well as the accessory passenger seat. It was a gift in 1978 from the Motor Company to retiring AMF chairman Rodney Gott, who had learned to ride motorcycles on a VL in the military. Gott gifted it back to the company in 1980, which used it for many years afterward for parades, public appearances, and in motion picture projects. The standard VLD sold for $320, and the price of the sidecar was $105.

1934 Model VLD

"Fighting Bob' Fitzsimmons was famous for his punch. So is the 1934 Harley-Davidson.

"Benny Leonard has the Punch that Wins. So has the 1934 Harley-Davidson.

"Frank Gotch has the Power that Wins—so has the 1934 Harley-Davidson.

"Jim Corbett had a Fighting Heart. So has the New Harley-Davidson.

"Like 'Gentleman Jim' Corbett, this great TNT motor doesn't know the meaning of 'quit.' No matter how hard the going, its never-say-die power keeps punching away. A true FIGHTING HEART—like all CHAMPIONS have!"

—Harley-Davidson advertisement

According to period advertising, the 74-cubic-inch flathead "T.N.T. Motor" in Harley-Davidson's 1934 Model VLD offered "explosive performance with outstanding reliability." To promote this potent engine, the company launched an advertising campaign called the "Fighting Heart," which featured the best boxers and wrestling champions of the day.

The company produced 4,527 Model VLDs in 1934.

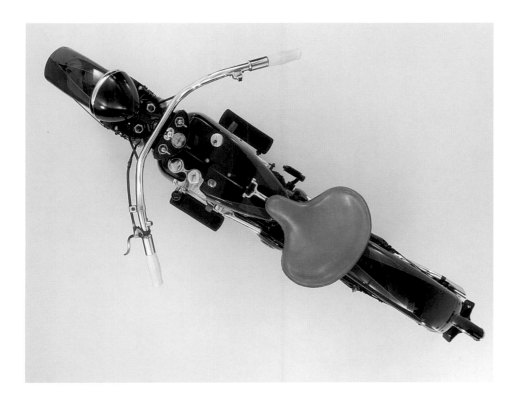

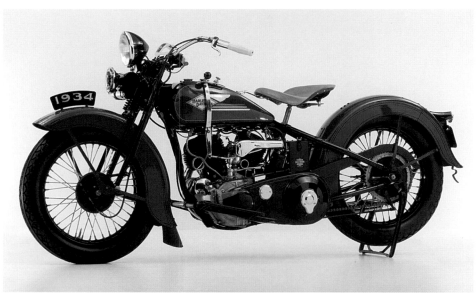

Frank Gotch had the **POWER THAT WINS**
—*so has the* 1934 HARLEY-DAVIDSON

The Motorcycle with the FIGHTING HEART

FRANK GOTCH, Wrestling Champion of the World, had the *power* that wins — and the *speed* — and the *fighting heart*.

So has the Harley-Davidson 74 Twin. Its new TNT motor delivers 36 horsepower! Realize what that means in getaway, speed, and pull. A true Fighting Heart, it never knows what "quit" means. Give it a stiff grade or deep mud to wrestle with and it's happy!

Treat yourself to a ride on this great motorcycle. Feel the thrill of its amazing performance. Notice its good looks, too—Airflo styling, low-swung grace, and rich color combinations. Be sure to ask your Harley-Davidson dealer about his Easy-Pay Plans. You'll never miss the price, or the low upkeep!

MAIL THIS COUPON →

Harley-Davidson Motor Co., Dept. P.,   Milwaukee, Wis.
Interested in the "Fighting Heart." Send illustrated literature.
Postage Stamp is enclosed to cover cost of mailing.

Name

Address

My age is ( ) 16-19 years,   ( ) 20-30 years,   ( ) 31 years and up,
( ) under 16 years.   Check your age group.

1934 Model C

"Those interested in motorcycles lighter in weight than the Twins—machines exceptionally economical in operation and easy to handle, will find remarkable values in the three single-cylinder models offered for 1934," proclaimed a brochure advertising Harley-Davidson's 1934 lineup. Its $187.50 B used a 21-cubic-inch (350cc) side-valve engine. The C, a more deluxe version selling for $225, made use of the company's 30.5-cubic-inch (500cc) single.

This model year marked the end of the Motor Company's production of singles for the U.S. market until 1948. By fall of 1934, the singles had disappeared from domestic price lists; however, the Motor Company continued to manufacture the Ricardo-head 21s for European and Asian markets until sometime in 1936. In addition, the company produced the Cs and the 30.5-cubic-inch engines until 1937.

Lacking a Model C in its collection, the Archives purchased this vehicle from a private collector. A survivor that probably passed through many owners during its lifetime, each adding his or her personal touches, the resulting motorcycle required a complete restoration makeover. This is the only vehicle in the collection with the optional cadmium rims, which cost an additional $1.00. The motorcycle is finished in Olive Green and black.

1935 Model R

After ceasing to market its single-cylinder motorcycles in the United States following the 1934 model year, the Motor Company introduced the Model R, with its 45-cubic-inch, low-compression V-twin engine to serve as Harley-Davidson's entry-level motorcycle for U.S. buyers.

Buying an entry-level motorcycle did not necessarily mean buying a plain, utilitarian transportation device. The Motor Company observed its dealers' and customers' activities, and it inaugurated "Special Equipment Groups" on order forms for 1935. These consisted of clusters of commonly ordered items. The Deluxe Solo Group, for example, provided safety guard, jiffy stand, 100-mile-per-hour speedometer, ride control, steering damper, stop light. fender light, dice shifter knob, dice switch keys, saddle bags, and special chrome plating for the package price of $49.50. Police Group No. 1 offered the safety guard, jiffy stand, 100-miles-per-hour calibrated and hand-lighted speedometer, and rear wheel siren for $49.90.

The company produced 543 of the 1935 Model R motorcycles, selling them for $295 apiece. The paint is Teak Red and black.

1935 Model VLD

The company placed strong emphasis on its 45- and 74-cubic-inch side-valve twins even as it put the finishing touches on a new generation of engines and motorcycles for 1936. This Big Twin 74 had matured into a nearly flawless machine through upgrades and improvements over its lifetime. The company also introduced an optional four-speed transmission, though most of the product line shipped with tried-and-true three-speeds. One engineering innovation took on a styling significance: new gas-deflecting exhaust tips, soon dubbed "fish tails," added an ear-catching finish to the company's recognizable exhaust note.

This Venetian Blue motorcycle does not have a vehicle identification number. Overall company sales figures reached 10,398 in 1935, of which 3,963 were the $320 VLD models.

1936 Model VLH

"One glance and you will see that Harley-Davidson engineers have done things to the heads and cylinders of the 1936 models that set them apart from all their predecessors. Deeper fins and many more of them mean that engine heat is carried off more rapidly. Better cooling is the result and that means better motor performance, longer motor life, additional service-free miles!"

—Harley-Davidson advertisement

This VLH Sport Solo introduced the Motor Company's 80-cubic-inch Big Twin engine. This example may have been an early running prototype because it incorporates flat side tanks decorated with the later "Flying Wheel" tank logo. To address engine cooling challenges, the engineers redesigned cylinders and heads. Production reached 2,046 of these VLH 80 models for the 1936 model year. Both this Sport Solo version and the lower-compression sidecar Model VHS sold for $340.

1936 Model VLH Police Solo

"The time to reduce the death-and-injury toll is RIGHT NOW!... Remember—proper patrols prevent violaters from getting by with their vicious driving habits. Clamp down on 'em and clamp down hard!"

—Harley-Davidson advertisement

The VLH Sport Solo used an 80-cubic-inch flathead engine mounted in a single-downtube frame. This example has a three-speed hand-shift transmission with a stronger, convex gear-shift lever, though the company had introduced its four-speed transmission as a $15 option by this time.

This police-specification motorcycle, painted black and white, included the 100-miles-per-hour speedometer ($36), receive-only radio with antenna and speaker ($85), foot-operated siren ($25), first-aid kit ($9.30), billy club, flashlight, tire pump, fire extinguisher ($15), and windshield with canvas leg covers. This example had 51,524 miles on it when it joined the Archives collection. The company manufactured 2,046 VLH models in 1936, selling them for $340.

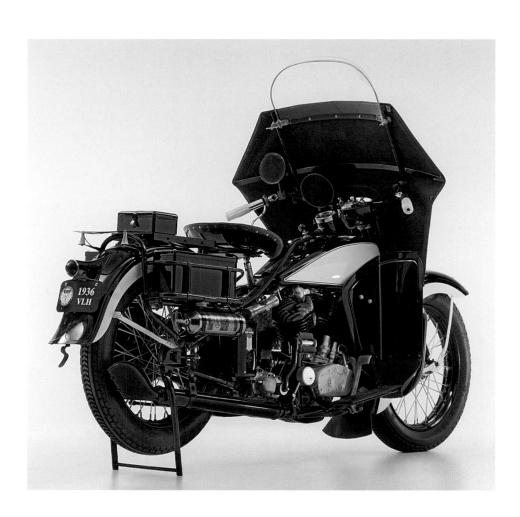

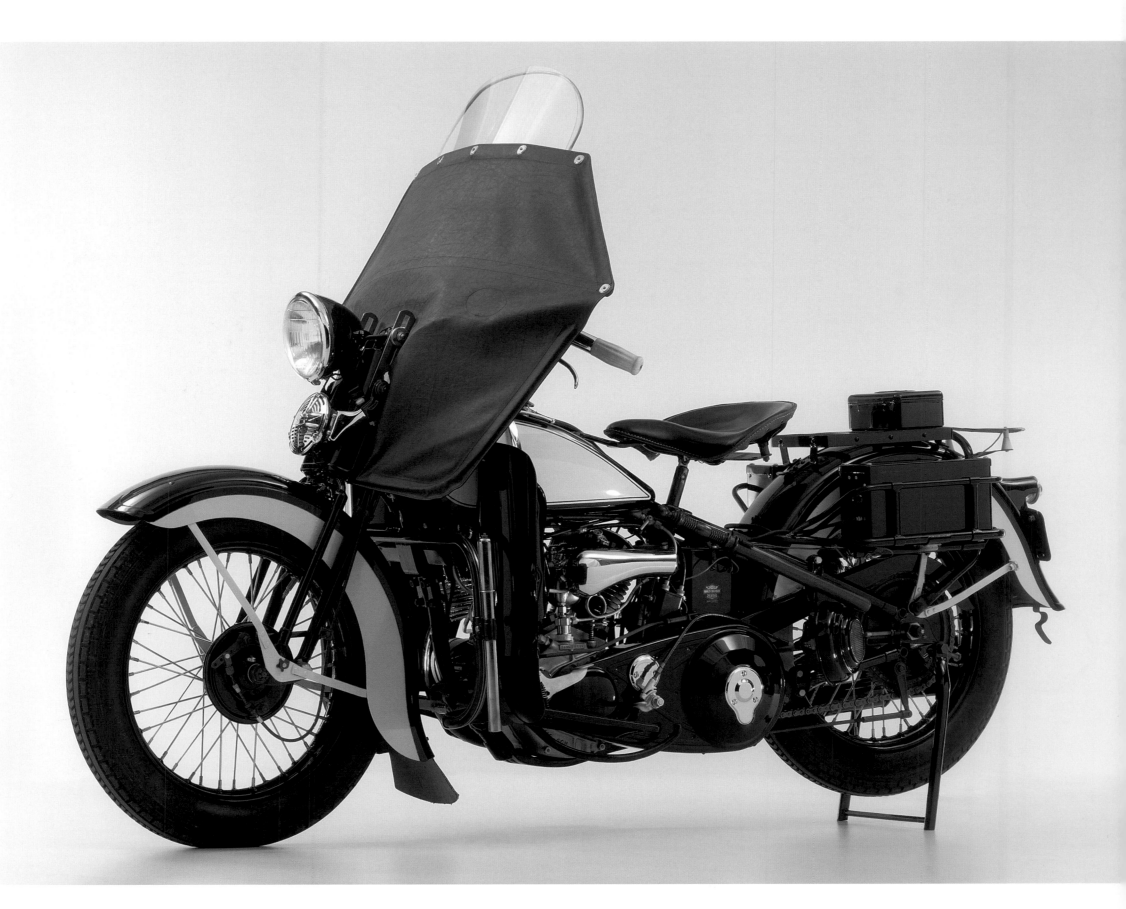

1936 Model GD Servi-Car

"Speedy auto pickup and delivery with Servi-Car! Garage men, super-service men—make it easy for auto owners to have you do their work. With this economical one-man pickup and delivery you can call for and deliver cars anywhere in the city or suburbs. Save your customers bother and inconvenience—get their good will and steady patronage. Investigate today. Give us a call and we will come right over and tell you the story."

—Harley-Davidson advertisement

By 1936, customers had begun to see the utilitarian value of the Servi-Car, even though Harley-Davidson built just 96 examples for that model year. Advertising and promotional literature highlighted the numerous roles this versatile machine could play, such as pickup and delivery for service-oriented businesses and traffic control for police departments. This Croydon Cream (a period-correct color) and Buick Blue example is painted in the livery of Thompson Motors, a Milwaukee Buick dealership in 1936.

1937 Model UH

The 1937 Model UH was among the first of the redesigned 80-cubic-inch side-valve models with deeper cooling fins, an upright timer on the gear case cover, and a Linkert carburetor. These medium-compression models incorporated the appearance cues of the 1936 EL, with its double-downtube frame, wraparound oil tank, teardrop instrument panel (with speedometer, ammeter, oil pressure gauge, and ignition and light switches), and skirted fenders. While the oil tank on this example is black, typically the factory painted them to match the gas tank. The company assembled just 185 UH models in 1937. They sold for $415.

1938 Model WLD

This was the "Sport Solo—Extra High Compression" 45-cubic-inch twin from the 1938 model year lineup. The WLD replaced the earlier R models. It incorporated all the innovations of the recently introduced overhead-valve EL model, including the single-loop frame, rounded gas tank, and teardrop instrument panel. The company made the front fender light standard equipment. This motorcycle uses a Linkert carburetor.

Harley-Davidson produced 402 examples of the WLD, selling them for $355 apiece. This color is called Venetian Blue.

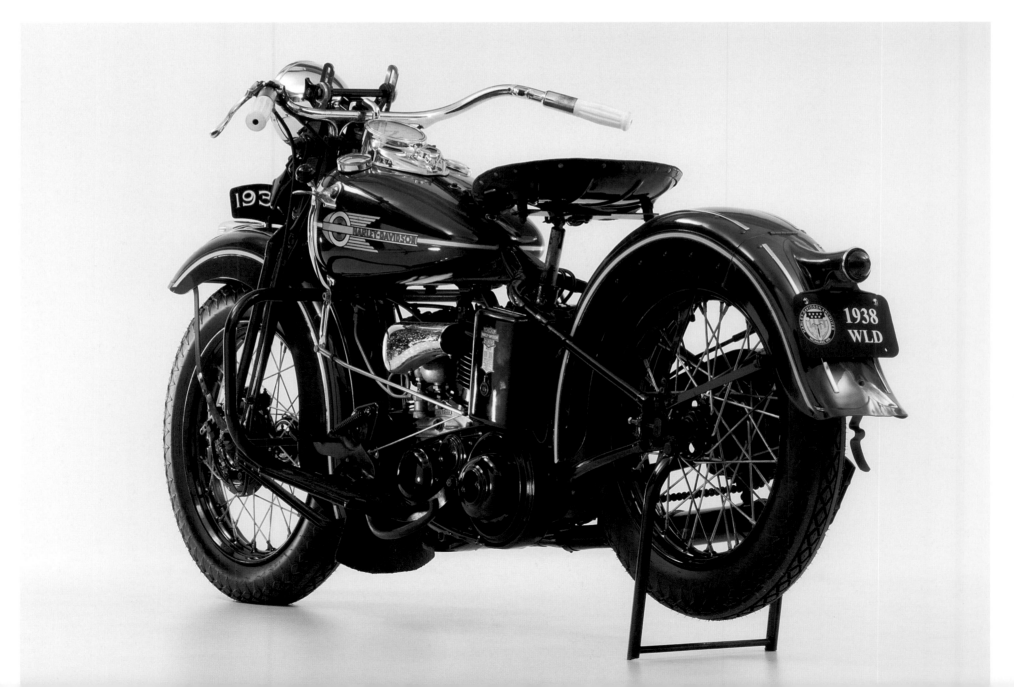

1939 Model ULH

The ULH was the 80-cubic-inch Special Sport Solo model, equipped with a four-speed, hand-shift transmission. This was the only year in which engineering placed the neutral position between second and third gears on the gearshift gate, and the "Cat's-Eye" instrument panel also debuted with this model year. The engine came equipped with new steel-strutted pistons that were horizontally slotted, and engineering fitted two-piece valve-spring covers.

Harley-Davidson produced 384 ULH models in 1939, and these sold for $415. The color scheme is black and ivory.

1939 Model G Servi-Car

John A. Stanton of Babylon, New York, purchased this Servi-Car new in 1938 for use in his Dodge-Plymouth dealership as a pickup and delivery vehicle. The license plate indicates the last year the bike was registered was 1948. This vehicle bears the original paint, along with lettering from the automobile dealership that is still legible on the fenders and box. This Servi-Car has 12,065 miles and is one of 320 Model Gs with the standard-size Commercial Body that the factory produced. John Stanton's daughter, Judith Scandura of Cortez, Florida, and her son, John Jr., donated this Servi-Car (painted Teak Red and black) to the Archives in January 1998.

HARLEY-DAVIDSON
SERVI-CAR

THE GREATEST VOLUME AND SALES BUILDER IN THE AUTO-MOTIVE BUSINESS . . . .

6
"Sensation of the Motorcycle World"

The Knuckleheads: 1936–1947

The world's obsession with speed continued throughout the Great Depression, and as economic prosperity slowly returned, the reemerging motorcycle buyer demanded ever more performance from his or her machine.

The Harley-Davidson Motor Company was only too happy to oblige. Improvements in fuel distillation, particularly the addition of tetraethyl lead as an anti-knock agent that allowed the use of higher compression ratios, made the once-exotic overhead-valve configuration a practical proposition, setting the stage for the introduction of one of the most important motorcycle engines of all time: the Harley-Davidson Knucklehead.

1936 Model EL

"Minus fanfare and ballyhoo, a new motorcycle has come on the scene and has taken the world by storm. Wherever shown, wherever ridden and owned, the new 61 OHV Harley-Davidson has caused a sensation. Here is a NEW motorcycle incorporating ideas the seasoned motorcyclist gives his immediate and unqualified approval. As one owner writes, 'It's my dream come true.'

"From everywhere come the most enthusiastic praises for this super motorcycle. Its wonderful handling qualities, its snappy response, its ability to stand up and 'take it' make this 61 OHV the outstanding motorcycle of today and the motorcycle of tomorrow."

—Harley-Davidson advertisement

Completely new from the ground up, the 1936 EL—the Special Sport Solo model—introduced Harley-Davidson's first 61-cubic-inch, overhead-valve V-twin engine, which the company claimed produced 40 horsepower. The engine earned its nickname "Knucklehead" because of the rounded shapes of the rocker covers, which resembled a closed hand, knuckles up. This particular example has 112 miles on the odometer. It still has its original tires.

The company manufactured 1,526 examples of the EL model during 1936. The motorcycle sold new for $380.

1940 Model EL

Fitted with the Knucklehead engine, the 1940 Model EL motorcycles used a larger Linkert carburetor and increased cylinder-head porting to boost horsepower. For this model year, engineering changed the front-wheel brake drum to a casting in order to eliminate flexing and improve braking. The front fork was heat treated for the first time. Engineering also added ribbing to the crankcase housing and introduced the new round air cleaner. The new "Speedline" toolbox appeared, along with D-shaped footboards that replaced the long-lived rectangular ones. The Deluxe Sport Solo option group (a $47 package) included the chrome muffler and many other chrome trim pieces, such as headlight, handlebars, and instrument panel, the colored shift knob, and the deluxe saddlebags and saddle.

The company manufactured 3,893 of the EL models in 1940. This Flight Red example sold new for $430 plus the Sport Solo option group.

1941 Model FL with 1941 Model M Package Truck

"The Package Truck attaches to the 61, 74, and 80 Twins and provides a most speedy, economical delivery unit that will handle loads up to 500 pounds. The Package Truck gets through traffic with amazing ease, can be parked most anywhere and is high in advertising value."

—Harley-Davidson dealer bulletin

This 1941 FL featured the new 74-cubic-inch, overhead-valve Knucklehead engine. The displacement increase helped bump power output to 48 horsepower at 5,000 rpm, making the 74 better equipped to deal with the additional weight of the Package Truck than the 61-cubic-inch E series. Archives acquired this Package Truck in 1999 and rebuilt and restored it, replacing wood and sheet metal. In 2000, Archives staff painted it Motor Company orange and black and lettered and decorated the box to resemble an Archives delivery vehicle.

In 1941, the company assembled 2,452 FLs, and this model sold new for $465. The Package Truck added another $135.

1946 Model FL

"Go where there's fun—on a Harley-Davidson. Motorcycling—'the world's greatest sport'—is now at a new peak of popularity. In every section of the country—more motorcycle fans want Harley-Davidsons than ever before. Even with our production at an all-time high—dealers are selling Harley-Davidsons faster than we can produce them. That's why it's *important* to see your dealer EARLY—if you want the excitement, fun and thrills that go with owning a Harley-Davidson Motorcycle. Because . . . they're well worth waiting for until your dealer can make delivery of *your* Harley-Davidson!"

—Harley-Davidson advertisement

Harley-Davidson's early postwar advertising cited strong demand for the company's motorcycles as the reason customers had to wait for new machines like the popular overhead-valve FL, but in reality the shortage of raw materials also played a major role in slowing the production of civilian vehicles for the U.S. market. As part of the ambitious program for rebuilding war-ravaged European countries, those countries were given priority in the allocation of rubber, steel, and fuel at the expense of American manufacturers like Harley-Davidson.

1947 Model EL

The year 1947 marked the last year of production for the Knucklehead engine, which was again available as either a 74-cubic-inch Model FL or a 61-cubic-inch Model EL. Production of the overhead-valve Big Twins had been interrupted by World War II, but by 1947 Harley-Davidsor was once again producing significant numbers of the motorcycles for the civilian market, building 4117 Model ELs. This example has 323 miles on the odometer.

1947 Model FL

In 1947, the Special Sport Solo model had a new taillight, a tank name badge, black grips, and a front fork adjuster. With this model, the front fender light and rear safety guard were standard equipment, as was the rubber-mounted instrument panel. The 1947 FL introduced self-aligning head bearings and hydraulic shock absorbers (although buyers could purchase the motorcycle with the earlier-style Ride Control system for $7.50 less).

While this motorcycle has elements of the Special Solo Group—including deluxe saddlebags, chrome fender lamp, headlamp, and engine air cleaner—it also has a gray covered buddy seat, "Hollywood" handlebars, and a chromed front fork, toolbox, primary cover, and shift knob. The maroon-and-beige paint scheme was not a factory option, and Archives presumes that its previous owner had it repainted sometime during his ownership. The motorcycle has covered 14,968 miles, according to its odometer. The company assembled 6,893 FLs in 1947, and this motorcycle was priced at $604 plus an additional $100 for the Special Solo Group with hydraulic shock absorbers.

7

"Front Line Hero!"

The Flathead Military and K Models: 1941–1973

On December 7, 1941, about 360 Japanese warplanes swooped out of the western skies and surprised the America military personnel stationed at Pearl Harbor. The next day, Congress declared war on Japan. Three days after that, on December 11, the United States went to war against Italy and Germany. Nearly every industrial manufacturer in the United States went to work for the war effort, providing motorcycles, tanks, aircraft, ships, guns, bullets, uniforms, medical supplies, food, and fuel to fight what became a global war.

Like other U.S. manufacturing companies, the Harley-Davidson Motor Company answered the government's call and devoted its resources to supplying U.S. troops fighting in Africa, Europe, and Asia. The bikes built for the war effort would later provide the raw material for custom motorcycle builders around the world.

1942 Model WLA

Harley-Davidson built the Model WLA by the tens of thousands for the United States armed forces and their allies during World War II. The rubber pads on the footboards on this Archives example still show the Harley-Davidson name; however, this brand identification ended at about this time, when new government regulations prohibited brand names on military vehicles. Accordingly, Harley-Davidson promoted its role in World War II in understated ways:

"The present conflict emphasizes mechanization to a degree never dreamed of a few years ago . . . Harley-Davidson motorcycles are being called to the colors . . . as an integral part of this country's highly mobile forces that are an answer to foreign *Blitzkreig*. Here motorcycle reconnaissance units feel out the enemy, probe for traps, mines, and ambushes, secure bridges and establish points of strength. . . . Then they follow the tanks to crash through the enemy barricades. . . ."

All WLA models manufactured during World War II are labeled as 1942 models regardless of their year of manufacture. The Thompson .45-caliber submachine gun in this example's scabbard has been rendered non-functional. The motorcycle has a windshield with canvas apron, steel leg shields, and a blackout headlight. The Motor Company built 60,437 WLA models in military and civilian specification between 1940 and 1945, as well as another 17,823 WLC sidecar versions. Records indicate that the factory manufactured this particular example in 1945. Civilian price would have been $380; the government contract price was $379.84.

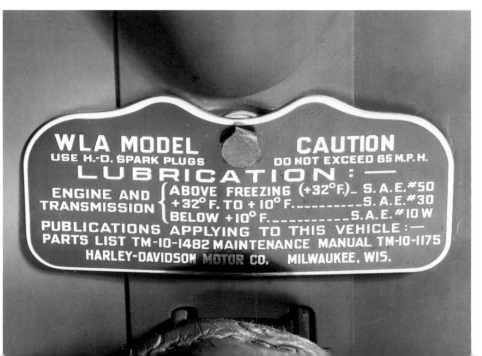

WLA MODEL   CAUTION
USE H.-D. SPARK PLUGS   DO NOT EXCEED 65 M.P.H.
LUBRICATION :—
                              ⎧ ABOVE FREEZING (+32°F.) _ S.A.E. #50
ENGINE AND   ⎨ +32° F. TO + 10° F. _____ S.A.E. #30
TRANSMISSION   ⎩ BELOW +10° F. _____ S.A.E. #10W
PUBLICATIONS APPLYING TO THIS VEHICLE :—
PARTS LIST TM-10-1482 MAINTENANCE MANUAL TM-10-1175
HARLEY-DAVIDSON MOTOR CO.   MILWAUKEE, WIS.

1942 Model XA

At the beginning of World War II, the United States government requested that Harley-Davidson produce a vehicle for operation in sandy terrain. The company developed the Model XA, a shaft-driven motorcycle with a horizontal, 750cc opposed-twin engine generating 23 horsepower. This particular example bears serial number 42XA1001, the first of the series. Many of its components appear to have been modified or fabricated during the vehicle's development. Engine guards, exhaust pipes, and skid plate do not resemble those on other Harley-Davidson XA models. Archives staff believes this particular motorcycle was the vehicle the U.S. Army evaluated prior to making its order official.

Harley-Davidson manufactured a total of 1,011 units of the Model XA before the army cancelled orders for the motorcycle. The XA introduced the company's first foot-shift transmission, an innovation that Harley-Davidson would carry over to its products after the war. Records indicate the price for these motorcycles was $870.35. This example had 3,450 miles on the odometer when it reached the Archives collection.

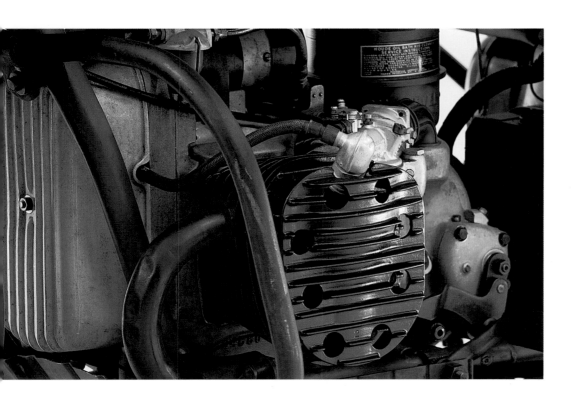

1942 Model XS with Sidecar

Archives records suggest the company assembled only three XS sidecar versions of the Model XA. The rear wheel of the motorcycle drove an axle that ran beneath the sidecar to provide additional traction in sandy or rough terrain. While its serial number classifies it as an XA, photos of the experimental unit label this particular example as the XS model. Engineering fitted it with heavily cleated, tractor-type tires for traction in sand.

This example has dual scabbards, with a Thompson .45-caliber submachine gun and a non-functioning M-1 carbine. It also is equipped with a field radio, a canteen, signal flags, a mess kit, a shovel, a passenger seat, a first-aid kit, and a U.S. Army–issue blanket. This example had 2,838 miles on its odometer when it reached Archives. Non-sidecar versions of the XA carried a price of $870 dollars, but no information exists to suggest a price for the powered sidecar.

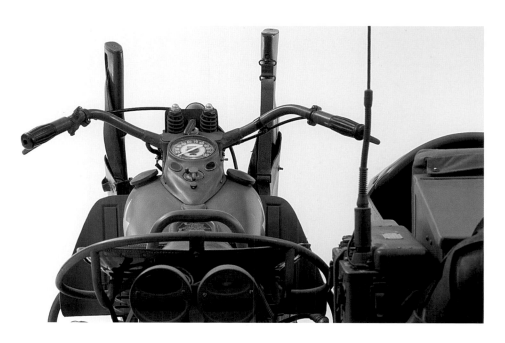

1942 Model U Navy with Sidecar

During the war, Harley-Davidson, which continued to sell motorcycles to the civilian population, promoted its products and wartime efforts through regular advertising that often included excerpts from letters the company received from soldiers serving on the Atlantic or Pacific fronts:

"No letter, among the thousands we have received, is more typically American than this one from Seabee 'Lefty' C-," one of the ads began.

"'When I was a civilian, I had a Harley-Davidson. Its performance was superb. Have shore duty here with the Navy Seabees. Harley-Davidsons are used for specialized duties and they never balk on the most rugged assignments. One of the freedoms I will feel I have earned will be to have a Harley-Davidson under me again and feel the good old American wind biting my face.'"

The Motor Company produced an unspecified number of its sidecar-equipped Model U's for use by U.S. Navy Shore Patrol and Seabee units use during World War II. This particular example has blackout lights, a siren, a tire pump, and the nomenclature badge. The sidecar has a step, a spare tire, and an M-1 Garand rifle in its leather scabbard.

1942 Model WLA "Russian" Boozefighters Cutdown Replica

This Archives replica faithfully represents the kind of early customizing that veterans did to personalize their own motorcycles after returning from World War II. When the museum team required a post–World War II cut-down for an exhibit on postwar motorcycle clubs, Archives restorers created this bike using the best parts of a pair of "civilianized" Russian bikes that had originally been sent overseas as part of the Lend-Lease program during World War II.

With club permission, Archives painted the bike in the green and white colors of the Boozefighters, one of the original postwar motorcycle clubs. They created an authentic recreation of a genuine Boozefighters bike, right down to the club's three-star bottle insignia painted on the battery box.

1947 Model G Servi-Car

The Milwaukee Police Department acquired this 1947 Model G Servi-Car new. In 1992, when Archives purchased the motorcycle, it was complete but required total restoration. Staffers installed new piston rings, straightened the frame, and replaced paint, plating, and tires. This Police Silver Model G sold new for $710 plus the $75 Police Group, including skid plate, rear-wheel siren, trip odometer, chrome bumper, and chalk stick for marking parked car tires. This silver color was available only to police customers. The factory assembled 1,307 of the Model Gs in 1947.

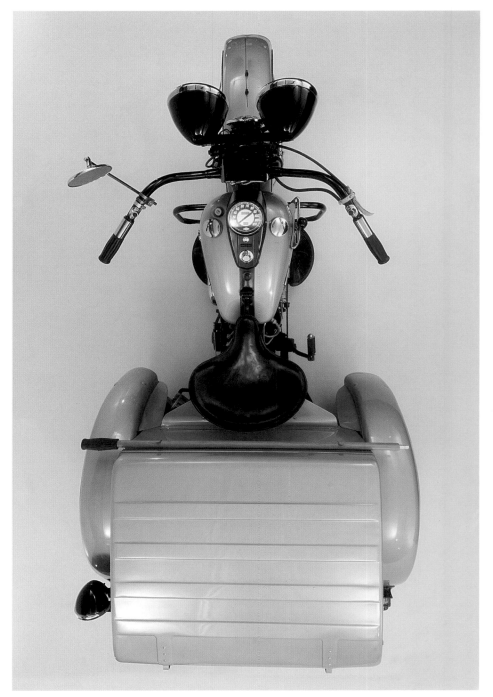

1952 Rikuo

Sankyo Pharmaceuticals manufactured Harley-Davidson motorcycles in Japan beginning in the late 1930s using tooling that the Motor Company sold them. Under the name Rikuo, Japanese for "King of the Land," Sankyo resumed motorcycle manufacture in 1950 following World War II. The company produced both 45- and 74-cubic-inch flathead models. This example uses a 45-cubic-inch engine with three-speed foot-shift transmission. This particular example contains an eclectic mix of components, including a late-1930s-style engine and a 1949-era front fork similar to the one used on the Hydra-Glide. There is no way to determine production numbers or original selling price. Archives is also uncertain of the originality or correctness of the example shown.

1952 Model K

The 1952 Model K was Harley-Davidson's first completely new motorcycle since the company introduced the E and EL Knuckleheads in 1936. A 45-cubic-inch, 750cc side-valve engine developing approximately 30 horsepower drove the K. With its integral four-speed transmission, foot shift, and hand clutch, it was the company's most technologically advanced vehicle up to that time. The engine incorporated removable aluminum heads and aluminum-alloy pistons. This bike also introduced Harley-Davidson's first hydraulically damped swing-arm rear suspension.

Harley-Davidson manufactured 1,970 of the Model K Sport 45. This color was called Metallic Bronco Bronze and was a $10.30 option. The motorcycle in standard colors sold for $865.

NEW
Brilliant and
Beautiful

1954 Model KH

"For the riding thrills of your life, ride the Harley-Davidson KH. Hold on to your hats—get ready—get set for the most thrilling time of your life—when you take your first ride on the new, power-packed 55 cu. in. Model KH! Mere words cannot describe the surging speed, the terrific dig-out, the amazing performance of the KH—you've got to ride it and see for yourself! There is nothing like it in the world. It's different, it's new, it's great! See it—ride it today!"

—Harley-Davidson advertisement

Period advertising for the 1954 Model KH responded to complaints that the earlier Model K had been underpowered. To create the "power-packed" KH, engineering enlarged the side-valve engine to 55 cubic inches. While not yet "terrific," the "dig-out" of the enlarged engine was much improved.

Just as with all 1954 models, the company commemorated its 50th anniversary with a 2.5-inch-diameter, gold-colored medallion mounted on the front fender. The company assembled 1,579 of the KH Sport models in 1954. This Anniversary Yellow model sold for $925.

1956 Model KH

In January 1956, Elvis Presley purchased this new Pepper Red and white Model KH from Memphis, Tennessee, dealer Tommy Taylor. Papers in the Archives collection indicate that Presley paid $903.19, including the trade-in amount from his S-series 165cc Harley-Davidson. He then made payments of $47 a month. Full list price for the KH would have been $925 plus $75.75 for the Deluxe Group. The buddy seat cost an additional $18, plus $15.25 for the windshield. The grand total for this motorcycle was $1,034, leaving Presley's trade-in worth about $110.

Elvis appeared on the cover of the May 1956 issue of *The Enthusiast* aboard this KH. When he decided to upgrade to a 1957 FL, Presley gave this motorcycle to his riding buddy, Fleming Horne. Horne rode the bike for a few years, then restored it and put it in his own collection. In early 1995, Archives acquired the motorcycle from Horne.

The company manufactured 539 of these in 1956.

1971 Model GE Servi-Car

Though the Servi-Car's 45-cubic-inch flathead and three-speed hand-shift transmission with a reverse gear were thoroughly antiquated by 1971, the year this example was built, the versatile three-wheeler continued to be popular with police departments across the United States. In fact, Servi-Cars continued to perform official duties for many years after production ceased in 1973. The GE used a Hydra-Glide front fork, which had replaced the earlier springer-type fork in the late 1950s, and featured an electric starter, which had been added for the 1964 model year.

When Archives acquired this vehicle from a collector in Massachusetts, it was clear that this Servi-Car had been a police vehicle, although no one could determine which department used it. In 2000, Archives cleaned and restored this motorcycle to resemble a Chicago Police Department vehicle from the period. Staffers painted the fork and nacelle black, repainted the wheels, and installed a new fiberglass box. Restorers affixed Chicago PD decals as well as the correct message easel and a blue rotating beacon light.

Harley-Davidson manufactured 500 GEs in 1971. The vehicle's original purchase price was $2464.30.

8

"Beats Anything on Two Wheels"

Intermediate Race Bikes: 1932–1958

Motorcycle racing helped the population of the United States recover from a crippling economic depression, distracted it from worrying about its young men fighting overseas during the war, and provided a much-needed outlet for those same young men once they returned home.

Indian Motorcycles, Harley-Davidson's main racing competitor in the prewar era, vanished during this period, but as the era wound down European motorcycles began to fill the void left by Indian's departure from dirt track racing at fairgrounds around the nation. Small Japanese motorcycles even began competing against the big, powerful Harley-Davidsons of the period, though they weren't taken very seriously at first.

1932 Model DAH Factory Hillclimber

The first DAH competition models appeared in 1929. Archives records suggest that the factory assembled about 25 examples in various configurations. Curiously, it seems that all the examples got vehicle identification numbers beginning with "30" as the year of manufacture, although this particular motorcycle is a later machine. This is one of only two surviving motorcycles that feature the double-downtube frame that factory racer Joe Petrali used to win the National Hill Climb Championship in 1932.

Not only does this motorcycle have its original double-downtube frame, but the motor, racing handlebars, tanks, and front fork are original and correct. This racer had a special spark-advance mechanism mounted on the handlebar near the ignition kill switch, and it competed with a racing transmission.

1935 Model VLD Hillclimber

Archives staffers believe this VLD may have started life as a street motorcycle and then been modified by a previous owner to run as a hillclimb competitor. It uses a 74-cubic-inch (1,200cc), side-valve flathead engine with a hand-shift transmission. The owner/racer "bobbed" the fenders—that is, trimmed them short—fitted turned-down handlebars, put chains on the rear tire, and used a large overlay sprocket.

This machine's racing history is largely unknown.

1936 Model EL Record Bike

Harley-Davidson built this streamlined EL model to demonstrate the power and performance of its new 61-cubic-inch, overhead-valve Knucklehead engine. This particular motorcycle, with its disk front wheel, streamlined front forks, tiny front fairing (made from half of a gas tank,) and enclosed and tapered rear cowl, may represent the first use of streamlining in the United States for motorcycle speed-record purposes. Engineering equipped the engine with dual carburetors for this run, and a fuel mixture of alcohol and benzoyl boosted output to 65 horsepower at 5,700 rpm. The company determined that the hard-packed sand at Daytona Beach was the best venue for the land-speed-record attempt and tapped factory race team member Joe Petrali to ride.

During several practice runs, Petrali experienced a high-speed wobble. Engineers on the scene suspected that the streamlined body was the cause, so they removed it and taped a conventional seat onto the rear frame members. The modification did the trick: on March 13, 1937, Petrali broke the existing 1926 record of 132 miles per hour with a two-way run average speed of 134.83. But he wasn't finished. Feeling that the engine could go faster, he made another attempt. E. C. Smith, the American Motorcycle Association official on the scene, sent the Motor Company a Western Union telegram the next morning with the news:

"JOE PETRALI BROKE AMERICAN STRAIGHTAWAY RECORD TODAY ON SIXTY ONE OVERHEAD STOP BOTH WAYS AT MEASURE MILE ELECTRICALLY TIME STOP NORTH RUN 26.07 SOUTH RUN 26.80 STOP 136.185 MILES PER HOUR STOP . . . OFFICIALLY CERTIFIED AMERICAN MOTORCYCLE ASSN. . . ."

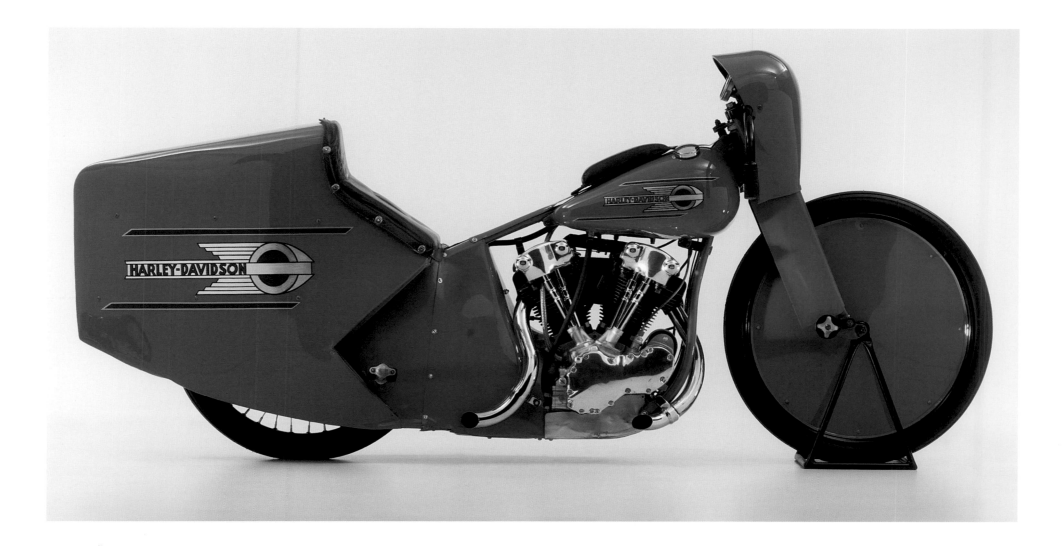

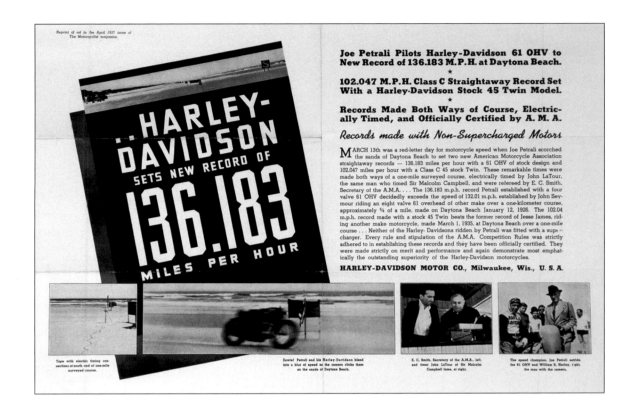

1953 Model KRTT Road Racer

This 1953 Model KRTT earned the "1" on its fairing through competition at road-racing courses across the United States. Factory team member Fred Nix originally raced this example, and Cal Rayborn raced it at Sears Point in 1969.

The race department tuned this 45-cubic-inch, side-valve flathead with dual Tillotson carburetors to develop 48 horsepower at 7,000 rpm and 50 ft-lb of torque at 5,000 rpm. As was the case with other factory racing motorcycles at the time, the vehicle identification prefix number—53—does not always mean the factory assembled it that year.

1958 Model XLCH

"Riding in the *'rough stuff'* is right up the Sportster's alley. Hills, sand or mud make no difference! 55 cubic-inch engine pulls you through in a breeze . . . takes the work out of *off the road* riding."

—Harley-Davidson advertisement

In 1958 Harley-Davidson introduced the XLCH, a high-compression performance version of the Sportster. With this model, Harley introduced the "peanut" gas tank originally used on the American lightweight models from 1948 to 1966 as well as staggered dual exhaust pipes, elements that remained as staples in the Sportster lineup well into the twenty-first century. The Motor Company equipped the XLCH with cut-down fenders and Goodyear Grasshopper tires and excluded all lighting and instrumentation, emphasizing the off-road capabilities of this machine. The company built only 239 XLCH models in 1958.

9

"A New Motorcycle for the Man of Action!"

The Panhead Era: 1948–1965

Technological improvements came at a breakneck pace throughout World War II. After the war, companies like Harley-Davidson applied many of these new technologies to vehicles built for an anxious population with pent-up desires. Harley-Davidson's new Panhead engine spoke to riders and buyers looking for engineering advances and styling improvements.

The world became a smaller place in the years after the war. High-flying airplanes, some even powered by jet engines, transported people across continents and oceans in hours instead of days, and a new interstate system provided magnificent new highways, highways of which the Harley-Davidson's new Panhead would soon be king.

1948 Model FL

"Do you like to roam? Does a winding road fascinate you with its alluring promise of some-thing new around every bend? Do you enjoy country air, the fragrance of fields, meadows, woodlands? Do tumbling waterfalls, quiet lakes, broad rivers bring you back to them again and again? Then you'll like motorcycling, world's greatest sport! For it takes you places, out in the open, to scenic wonderlands, faraway cities, brings you the thrills of gypsy tours, race meets, hillclimbs, exciting vacations . . . makes every spare hour happier, healthier outdoor enjoyment. It's so easy to enjoy motorcycling, easier than you think to own a genuine Harley-Davidson. Why not get started now?"

—Harley-Davidson advertisement

There was no finer way to "get started" in the "world's greatest sport" than aboard the 1948 Harley-Davidson FL Special Sport Solo, with its new 74-cubic-inch "Pan-head" engine. The new high-compression V-twin engine incorporated aluminum cylinder heads, hydraulic valve lifters operating in an oil mist, and distinctive chrome-plated pan-shaped rocker-arm covers that gave the engine its nickname.

While this was the first year for the new engine, it was the last for the springer front suspension on the solo Big Twin models (although the company continued to use this suspension system on sidecar models through 1949). The company assembled 8,071 Panhead-powered motorcycles in 1948. This Flight Red example sold for $650 new.

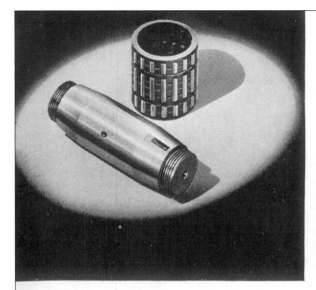

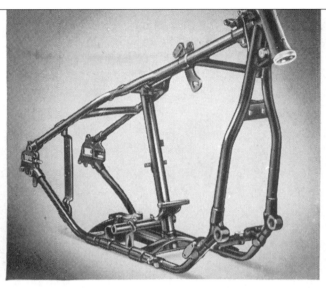

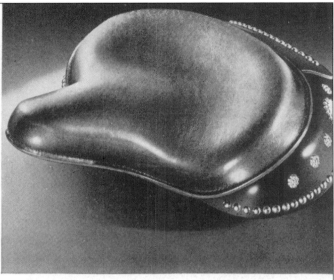

Big Twin crank pin features 54 roller bearings for longer, more satisfactory service.

Terminal box lugs and safety guard mounting plate incorporated on new Big Twin frames.

Extra-deep, latex-filled, de luxe solo saddle with jeweled, plastic skirt is now available.

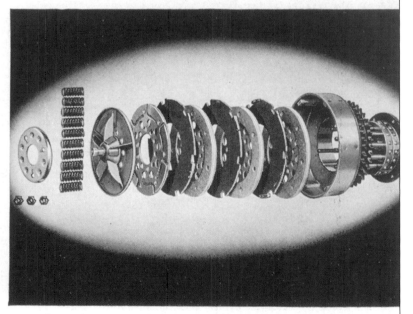

Bright chrome plating on tail lamp has been made available for 1948.

Redesigned, offset tow bar that keeps pace with new automobile advancements.

Smoother operation, longer life are advantages of the multiple dry disc clutch on all 1948 Big Twin Models.

1948 Model FL Custom

James M. Kobe purchased this Panhead new in 1948. Over the years he modified and personalized his bike. He converted it to a 12-volt electrical system with an alternator, giving him the juice to power the auxiliary taillights he added, as well as the additional lights inside the front wheel spokes. Kobe adapted a rear belt final-drive system from a Sportster to transmit power to the rear wheel. He gave the engine a complete overhaul in 1989 at 68,070 miles and installed new transmission bearings at that time. The odometer on this motorcycle turned over 100,000 miles just outside Milwaukee as Kobe rode it to the 95th anniversary celebration in June 1998. Total mileage read 100,148 in August 1998 when he presented it to the Motor Company.

Stock versions of this Azure Blue bike sold for $650 in 1948. Kobe added a variety of options to his bike at the time he purchased it. He reported to Archives staff members that he paid $965 for this motorcycle.

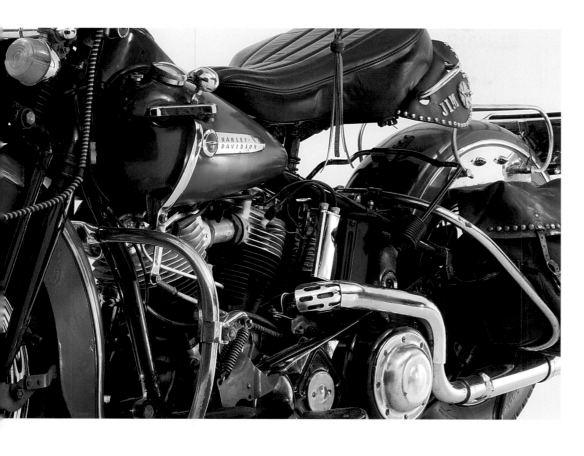

1949 Model FL Hydra-Glide

"Make yours a Hydra-Glide vacation! For the grandest vacation you ever had, swing into the saddle of a Hydra-Glide Harley-Davidson. Pack the saddle bags, take a friend on the buddy seat, fill up with gas and oil and you're off on a thrilling, fun-packed trip you will never forget. You'll ride all day and, if you wish, far into the night and still feel like going on and on."

—Harley-Davidson advertisement

In 1949, the Motor Company called on riders to hit the road and experience the comfort and safety of its newly introduced front suspension, featured on most Big Twin models. The Hydra-Glide front fork offered seven inches of shock absorption travel through a pair of hydraulic-oil-filled spring tubes. The sliding portions of this suspension were black for this year only. Company advertising explained the advantages offered by the new front suspension: "You'll glide over endless tar lines and over rough spots. You'll hit bumpy side roads and country lanes with barely a quiver. Gone is that feeling of fatigue. After a day of hundreds of miles of travel, you'll wake up the next morning fresh as a daisy—eager to get going and see more of this great country of ours."

The company manufactured 8,014 Hydra-Glide FLs in 1949. This Peacock Blue example sold new for $750.

10 REASONS WHY IT PAYS TO STICK *to* GENUINE HARLEY-DAVIDSON OIL

5 RESISTS DEEPEST FREEZE

At sub-zero temperatures, the Harley-Davidson Oil in your engine pumps instantly, providing instant flow of motor oil to vital engine parts . . . to cold, dry cylinder walls and pistons.

6 KEEPS PISTON RINGS FREE

Keeping piston rings free, resilient and "springy" is vitally important to the compression and power-seal of your engine . . . Harley-Davidson Oil keeps rings clean and free and efficient.

1 MADE EXPRESSLY FOR MOTORCYCLES

A lifetime of motorcycle engine lubrication experience has been poured into Genuine Harley-Davidson Oil . . . it pays off in every way, in power, in pep, in performance and in up-keep to use only Harley-Davidson Oil in your motorcycle.

2 PROVIDES "HAIR'S BREADTH" PROTECTION

The oil film that must seal the power, as well as resist the terrific heat and friction in your engine is not much thicker than a human hair . . . Harley-Davidson Oil is extra tough to provide positive, "hair's breadth" oil film protection.

3 RESISTS 3000 PISTON STROKES per MINUTE

At 60 miles per hour, the pistons in your motorcycle engine make 3000 strokes per minute . . . Harley-Davidson Oil assures positive protection and lubrication to both cylinder walls and pistons at all speeds.

7 RETARDS OXIDATION and CORROSION

Oxidation and corrosion are the birthplace of piston and bearing troubles and expensive repairs . . . Harley-Davidson Oil retards oxidation and corrosion . . . protects bearings and pistons.

8 MINIMIZES CARBON and SLUDGE

Sluggish engine performance and engine drag as well as power loss result when carbon, sludge and gum accumulate in your engine . . . the accumulation of these "barnacle-like" power robbers in your engine is retarded by Harley-Davidson Oil.

9 PROLONGS MOTOR LIFE

There's no greater insurance for longer, more powerful, prolonged new-engine performance than the use of Genuine Harley-Davidson Oil designed expressly for your motorcycle engine. You minimize repair expense . . . prolong the life of your engine . . . improve performance.

4 RESISTS CYLINDER TEMPERATURE OF 450°

450° F. . . . that's the temperature in your cylinders . . . that's the temperature Harley-Davidson Oil on the cylinder walls and pistons of your engine must stand up against.

10 Harley-Davidson values and wants your oil business, and knows that to deserve it, we must provide you with the finest motorcycle oil made.

The license plate on the rear fender reads:

HARLEY DAVIDSON ARCHIVES
MILWAUKEE, WIS.

1949
FL

1950 Model FL

Harley-Davidson's engineering team redesigned and enlarged the inlet ports in the company's 74-cubic-inch Panhead engine for 1950, resulting in a 10 percent increase in horsepower. Linkert carburetors and four-speed, hand-shift transmissions were standard on FL Solo models. Manufacturing used polished slider tubes on the Hydra-Glide front suspension. The newly introduced "Mellowtone" muffler produced a deeper exhaust note, and the saddle was redesigned to provide removable leather skirts and conchos. The left fuel tank held 2 gallons of gasoline, while the right tank accommodated 2.75 gallons. The oil tank held 1 gallon. This Riviera Blue example had 6 miles on the odometer when it joined the Archives collection.

The company assembled 7,407 FL Hydra-Glides in 1950. In spite of the improvements, the base price of a new FL remained at $750.

1954 Model FLF

In September 1954, Jackie Manouse of Newburgh, New York, purchased this 1954 Model FLF. He died a year later, and his fiancée purchased the bike. She stored it until 1971 and then sold it. A year later, Manouse's family reacquired the vehicle and stored it in Connecticut until 1992. Family members rode it briefly and then stored it again until 1995, when the Archives purchased it for the collection.

The second "F" in "FLF" refers to the foot-shifted transmission, which Harley-Davidson introduced as an option on Big Twin models for the 1952 model year. This example features the optional Deluxe Solo Group, which added a front-fender lamp, whitewall tires, a buddy seat, black leather saddlebags with white fringe, a luggage rack, front and rear auxiliary lights, a windshield, a centerstand, and chrome trim on both fenders. This motorcycle also has the Jubilee trumpet horn mounted on the right side.

The paint scheme on this particular motorcycle features a broad white horizontal stripe across the gas tank. This treatment did not appear in any literature; however, the previous owner claimed it was there at the time of purchase. Archives staffers have seen many other 1954 models with similar stripes, so they've concluded this may have been an unadvertised option.

The company produced 4,757 FLF models in 1954. Including the Deluxe Solo Group, a $46.60 option, Jackie Manouse paid $1,015 for this well-appointed Glacier Blue and white motorcycle in 1954.

1954 Model FLE Police Solo

"Here's a proven way to tighter traffic control during spring and summer's peak motoring. Mount your traffic officers on solo Harley-Davidsons. Motorists respect the speed, the maneuverability, the power that enables a motorcycle officer to apprehend violators . . . and they drive accordingly."

—Harley-Davidson advertisement

This Police-Silver unit uses a 74-cubic-inch Panhead engine with Harley-Davidson's three-speed hand-shift transmission with reverse gear, and it has the connections for sidecar use. The department that originally purchased this bike ordered the Traffic Combination, which installed special camshafts and a different carburetor for use in city traffic. This motorcycle has red and blue pursuit lamps ($17.25), a foot-operated siren ($36), a fire extinguisher ($15.40), a first-aid kit ($9.25), and a windshield. It is uncertain how many FLE Police units the company manufactured in 1954, but retail price with the Traffic Combination was $1,000.

1956 Model FLF

Harley-Davidson advertising proclaimed that the 74-cubic-inch Panhead offered riders "53-to-55 horsepower." The FLHF high-compression versions provided customers with a special high-lift cam and pistons, polished ports and bearings. and an 8:1 compression ratio. These higher-output models developed 58 to 60 horsepower.

This Pepper Red and White example has the Chrome Finish Group, a $54 option that included chromed front safety guard, rims, headlight, clutch cover, timing cover, inspection cover, exhaust pipe covers, and instrument panel cover. In addition, the option provided polished fork sliders, brake side cover, horn, and stainless-steel five-piece fork trim. This well-optioned motorcycle also has the buddy seat with rail, cigarette lighter, dual mufflers, windshield, and King Saddlebags, part of the $108 King of the Road option. The two-tone paint and chrome gas tank nameplate were standard equipment.

This motorcycle was one of 1,578 FLF models manufactured during 1956. It sold for $1,055 plus $162 for additional options.

1957 Model XL Sportster

"A new motorcycle for the man of action. . . . All the exciting riding experience you've ever dreamed of . . . all wrapped up in the sweetest chrome-and-enamel power package ever produced . . . the new Harley-Davidson overhead . . . the SPORTSTER! . . . Engineering, design and performance that will make you forget the riding thrills of yesterday and have you eagerly looking forward to the next ride on your new SPORTSTER."

—Harley-Davidson advertisement

The radical new Sportster introduced in 1957 would define Harley-Davidson performance for generations to come. While the frame and running gear evolved from the KH models, the new XL featured Harley-Davidson's first 55-cubic-inch, overhead-valve engine with an integral four-speed, foot-shift transmission. Like the KH, the new XL incorporated a telescopic front fork and rear swinging arm suspension. Like the front fork, the rear shock absorbers were hydraulically dampened. The XL engine used cast-iron cylinders, ran at 7.5:1 compression, and developed 40 horsepower at 5,500 rpm.

The color of this particular example was not listed on order blanks, so Archives staff have surmised this gold and white combination was not a standard color. This was the first year for the round, plastic tank badges. These inaugural Sportsters were unpopular with magazine reviewers and some buyers who criticized the bikes for being too slow. Small valves restricted the flow of fuel and exhaust.

The company assembled 1,983 Sportsters this first year. The new price was $1,103.

NEW *LOOK*

NEW *POWER*

NEW *RIDING THRILL*

1958 Model FLH

"Now! The Greatest Motorcycle ever built. A New Concept in motorcycle enjoyment with Cyclonic Getaway . . . Cloud-Cushioned comfort. New swinging-arm rear suspension combines with Hydra-Glide front fork and spring-loaded seat post to make the Duo-Glide a miracle ride."

—Harley-Davidson advertisement

The Duo-Glide earned its name from its new swinging-arm rear suspension, with motion dampened by a pair of hydraulic shock absorbers.

In 1958, the Motor Company produced an unknown quantity of motorcycles in this green and white color combination for the Shriners. When the Shriners took delivery, the company found it had assembled 12 more than the organization wanted. Eleven of these unusual units went to dealers, while this final example

went into the Archives. Two-tone paint was standard on all FL models, but not in this custom combination. This example also has the optional Chrome Finish Group, as well as whitewall tires.

Harley-Davidson assembled 1,299 FLF models and 2,953 FLHF models in 1958. Each sold for $1,320 plus the options.

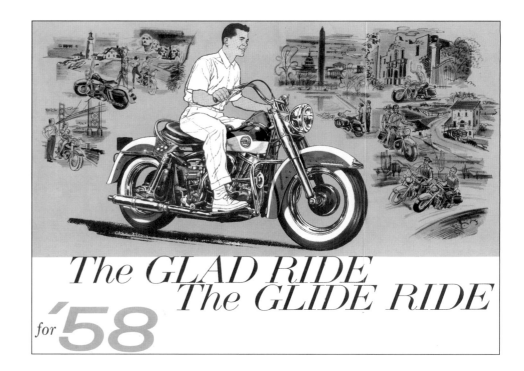

The GLAD RIDE
The GLIDE RIDE
for '58

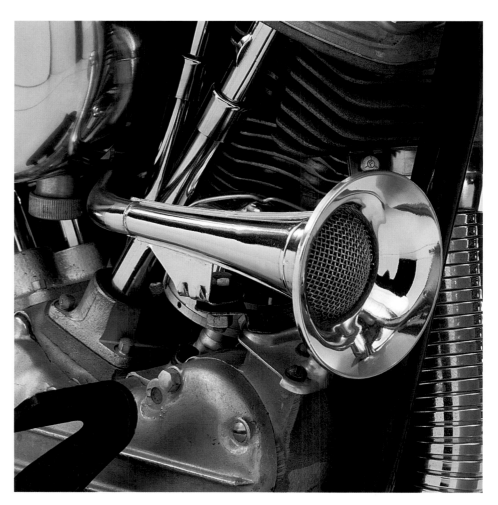

1957 Model FLH "Billy Bike" Replica

This is a replica of the motorcycle ridden by Dennis Hopper in the film *Easy Rider*. Actor Dennis Hopper played Billy, while co-star Peter Fonda played his friend, Wyatt. For the actual film, Fonda's film production company commissioned two identical motorcycles in this paint scheme. One was wrecked during filming, and the other disappeared and has never been located.

To create the bikes ridden by Hopper in the film, Fonda's fabricator extended and widened the forks on the FLH motorcycles, chromed the sliders, laced the wheels, and installed a short sissy bar, custom-made seat, chrome fenders and headlight, staggered dual exhausts, small-capacity custom gas tank, chrome oil tank, engine side covers, and chain guard. James Beck in Pomona, California, assembled this faithful re-creation of the Hopper bike. He made the air-cleaner cover from a distributor cover and formed the exhaust pipes and handlebars. The bike has no instruments.

1960 Model FLH
"Captain America" Replica

This is a replica of the motorcycle ridden by Wyatt, the character played by actor and producer Peter Fonda in the film *Easy Rider*. Fonda commissioned two identical heavily chromed motorcycles that his character was to ride during filming. During the dramatic final scene of the film, one of the originals was destroyed by fire. The other disappeared and has never been recovered.

To create this replica, fabricator Jim Beck of Pomona, California, worked with staff from the Otis Chandler Vintage Museum, which had earlier acquired 300 photographs of the motorcycle from the film. Later, with Fonda's assistance, they located individuals who had worked on the original motorcycles.

According to Fonda, this replica is faithful down to the buttons on the seat. Fonda's original motorcycle for the film used a 1962 FLH Police engine, while this replica has a 1960 version of the same. Beck upgraded the electrical system to 12 volts for dependability. He hid a regulator in the end of the generator housing to retain the look of the original 6-volt system.

Archives acquired this replica and the matching helmet in 1999.

1960 Model XLCH Sportster

"There's no substitute for cubic inches! MODERN OHV POWER. One twist of the throttle will tell you that you're packin' 55 cubic inches of dynamic horsepower. Take to the hills . . . take to the highways. No matter which model you ride, the SPORTSTER H or the CH, you've got power to spare. Ride it . . . try it . . . you'll buy it!"

—Harley-Davidson advertisement

By 1960, when this ad copy appeared, Harley-Davidson's Sportster had the beans to back up the advertising hyperbole. To address criticism that the XL engine had failed to perform, the 1959 and 1960 models received larger intake and exhaust valves, and the compression ratio was bumped to 9:1. The company offered two versions: the XLH for on-highway riding and this XLCH for road and off-road use. Engineering fitted high exhaust pipes to clear brush and offered a choice of tires for this model. The motorcycle hac a magneto spark-ignition system. Front and rear fenders were lighter weight than those on the XLH highway model. The only instrumentation offered was a speedometer. All of this combined to make the XLCH one of the highest-performing motorcycles sold in America in 1960.

The company sold this black and white XLCH for $1,310.

1962 Model FLHF Duo-Glide with LE Sidecar

The Motor Company kicked off promotions for the 1962 Panhead FL models with the slogan: "Sport for you—Sport for Two in '62!" The ad copy capitalized on the reputation for quality, comfort, and performance the Duo-Glide had earned since its 1958 debut: "Pair up on fun with DUO-GLIDE—the one motorcycle that has captured the hearts of pleasure riders the world over. It's the breathtaking beauty of American Craftsmanship. Superbly styled . . . designed for comfort . . . the peak of performance! On highway . . . expressway, or scenic country road the DUO-GLIDE

will give you sightseeing thrills in armchair comfort. It's built for you and fun for two. Sport-ride one today!"

This motorcycle had 10,138 miles on the odometer when Archives acquired it for the collection. The company manufactured 5,184 FL models in 1962. The FLHF in Hi-Fi Red and white sold for $1,400, while the Hi-Fi Red sidecar cost another $372.

1962 Model D-3 Golf Car

"Comparing scores is an 18th hole tradition. The same is true in golf car decision making. In the final tally, Harley-Davidson golf cars stand head and shoulders above all others. Tally up the scorecard yourself. See how many more value features Harley-Davidson golf cars offer as standard equipment."

—Harley-Davidson advertisement

Harley-Davidson entered the golf-car market in 1962 with two models, one powered by an electric motor and the other powered by a two-stroke, 250cc single-cylinder engine that used a fully automatic variable-speed transmission. The latter is shown here. Advertisements touted the two-stroke as "especially designed for golf-car operation . . . never talks above a whisper (especially when someone else is putting)."

Both versions used tubular steel frames and molded fiberglass bodies that hinged in the rear for access to the engine and drive components. Standard equipment included the dual bucket seats, tiller steering bar, cradle-type golf bag carriers, "high-flotation" tires, telescoping front-fork suspensions, removable tail gate, and disc brake that worked on the drive shaft. The gas version shown here measures 89.5 inches overall on a 59.5-inch wheelbase. It stands 36 inches tall with 4.6 inches of ground clearance, and it is 45.25 inches wide.

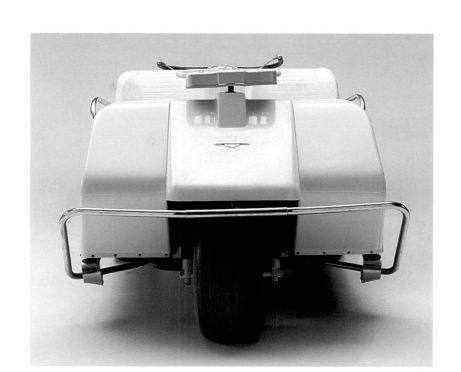

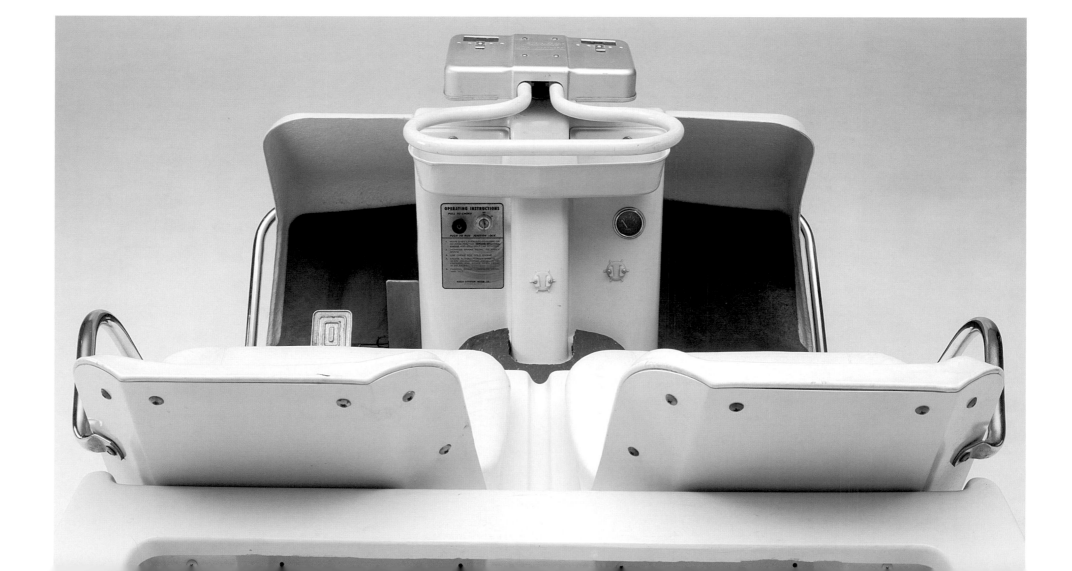

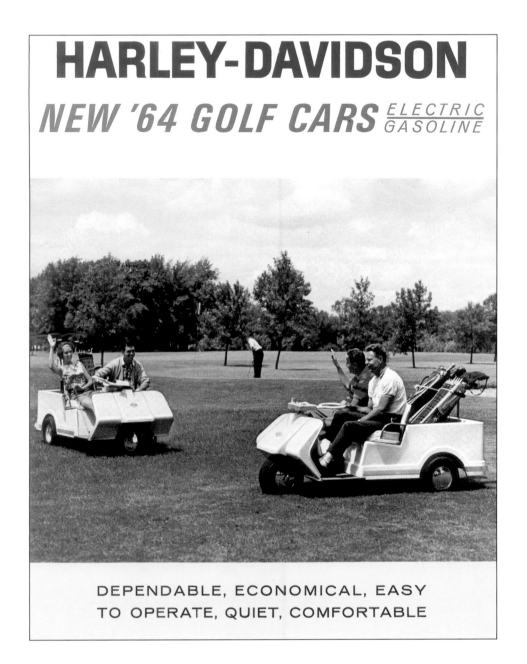

HARLEY-DAVIDSON
NEW '64 GOLF CARS ELECTRIC GASOLINE

DEPENDABLE, ECONOMICAL, EASY
TO OPERATE, QUIET, COMFORTABLE

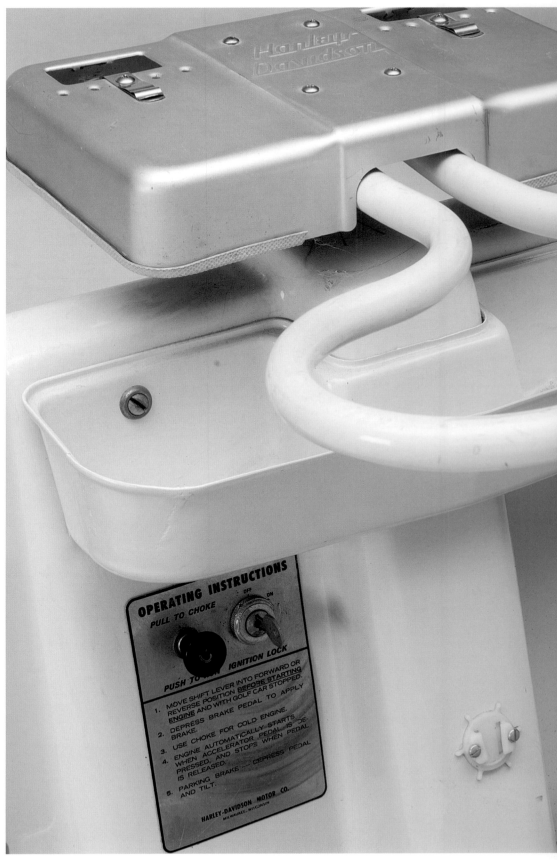

OPERATING INSTRUCTIONS

OFF ON

PULL TO CHOKE

IGNITION LOCK

PUSH TO RUN

1. MOVE SHIFT LEVER INTO FORWARD OR REVERSE POSITION BEFORE STARTING ENGINE AND WITH GOLF CAR STOPPED.

2. DEPRESS BRAKE PEDAL TO APPLY BRAKE.

3. USE CHOKE FOR COLD ENGINE.

4. ENGINE AUTOMATICALLY STARTS WHEN ACCELERATOR PEDAL IS DEPRESSED, AND STOPS WHEN PEDAL IS RELEASED.

5. PARKING BRAKE — DEPRESS PEDAL AND TILT.

HARLEY-DAVIDSON MOTOR CO.
MILWAUKEE, WISCONSIN

1965 Model FLHB Electra Glide with Model LE Sidecar

"Here it is!" The luxurious Big-Twin with an all-new Electric Starter. The Harley-Davidson Electra Glide—the Rolls-Royce of motorcycles—makes you and your machine the main attraction on any road 'round the world. There's miles of smooth riding for you—for two. Take a look—take a ride on an ELECTRA GLIDE!"

—Harley-Davidson advertisement

Harley-Davidson introduced electric start and a 12-volt electrical system in 1965. The primary drive on this particular 74-cubic-inch Panhead engine, which featured an optional three-speed, hand-shift transmission, incorporated the new cast-aluminum outer primary-case cover. The sidecar was equipped with a skirted windshield, step, and spare wheel with cover.

The company produced 4,800 FLH models in 1965. This Holiday Red FLHB sold new for $1,595, and the LE sidecar cost an additional $405. This example had 10,151 miles on the odometer when it reached Archives.

ALL NEW MODEL!!!
HARLEY-DAVIDSON
ELECTRA-GLIDE!

We've taken a few of the kicks away, but none we thought you'd miss. The new 1965 Electra-Glide has instant electric starting. You simply turn on the ignition and press the starting button. The result is sure-fire, instant starting in any weather. What's more, the new Electra-Glide has a 12-volt electrical system so you can add more electrical accessories than ever before.

instant
electric
starting

10

"Yours for Happy Days"

American Lightweights: 1948–1966

When the American soldiers returned to a newly prosperous country after World War II, they wanted nothing more than to raise families of their own, which they did in unprecedented numbers. Between the years 1946 and 1964, Americans had approximately 76 million children.

This "baby boom" generation provided a potential motorcycle market of unimaginable proportions, and Harley-Davidson was prepared to service that market with its line of small two-stroke motorcycles ranging in size from 125cc to 175cc. Whether a baby boomer wanted a Hummer, Topper, Scat, or Bobcat, Harley-Davidson had a machine to help young riders fulfill their two-wheeled dreams.

1948 Model S

"America's Newest Sensation On Wheels!. . . Here it is. . . everybody's motorcycle. . . a lightweight, sturdy, genuine Harley-Davidson that will take you places safely, quickly, conveniently and economically. Costs little to buy, little to operate. . . . Just the thing for going to and from work, school, store, town and on trips to distant places."

—Harley-Davidson advertisement

At the close of World War II, Harley-Davidson obtained rights to copy and produce the DKW 125cc single-cylinder two-stroke engine as part of the war reparations from Germany. The compact engine, which was mated to a three-speed foot-shift transmission, developed 1.7 horsepower. In mid-1948 the company introduced its first motorcycle powered by this engine, the Model S.

This bike had a wheelbase of 50 inches and a saddle height of 27.5 inches. The new "peanut" tank carried 1.875 gallons of gas/oil pre-mix. It returned 70 miles to a gallon of fuel and could reach 35 to 40 miles per hour. This example has an optional front engine guard and chrome wheels.

This was a tremendously successful introduction for Harley-Davidson. The company manufactured 10,117 of these lightweights, a figure that accounted for one-third of all Motor Company production for 1948. This bike sold for $325.

1948

America's Newest Sensation On Wheels!

Harley-Davidson 125

LIGHTWEIGHT, SINGLE CYLINDER; built by the world's largest manufacturer of motorcycles

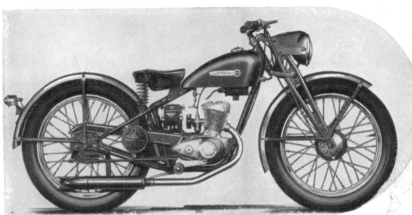

MOTORCYCLING FUN FOR EVERYONE

Personal Transportation at Low Cost!

Here it is . . . everybody's motorcycle . . . a lightweight, sturdy, genuine Harley-Davidson that will take you places safely, quickly, conveniently and economically. Costs little to buy, little to operate. Handles easily, rides comfortably. Just the thing for going to and from work, school, store, town and on trips to distant places. Miles of enjoyment at pennies of cost! Dependable personal transportation at real savings! See your Harley-Davidson dealer today and take a ride. Write for free illustrated literature.

HARLEY-DAVIDSON MOTOR CO., Dept. SM, Milwaukee 1, Wis.

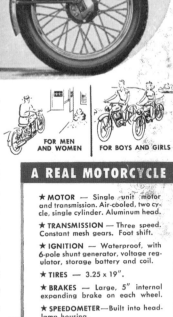

FOR MEN AND WOMEN   FOR BOYS AND GIRLS

A REAL MOTORCYCLE

★ **MOTOR** — Single unit motor and transmission. Air-cooled, two cycle, single cylinder. Aluminum head.

★ **TRANSMISSION** — Three speed. Constant mesh gears. Foot shift.

★ **IGNITION** — Waterproof, with 6-pole shunt generator, voltage regulator, storage battery and coil.

★ **TIRES** — 3.25 x 19".

★ **BRAKES** — Large, 5" internal expanding brake on each wheel.

★ **SPEEDOMETER**—Built into head-lamp housing.

1951 Model S

"Have Fun in '51. Beautiful, New and Exciting. The new Harley-Davidson 125 is the talk of the two-wheel world. You get all the former famous features . . . plus . . . road cushioning Tele-Glide fork . . . more power . . . bigger headlight . . . and a 'new look' from stem to stern. This you've got to see . . . and ride . . . and you'll want it!"

—Harley-Davidson advertisement

In 1951, Harley-Davidson restyled the S-series 125s, replacing the girder-style front suspension with a scaled-down version of the Hydra-Glide front suspension. Engineering created a new front fender and flared out the rear one. This Sportsman's Yellow S has 3 miles on the odometer as a result of being moved around the Vehicles Archives over the years; like many of the motorcycles in the collection, it had 0 miles when it joined the Archives.

The company assembled 5,101 of these lightweights, selling them for $365 apiece. The rear-fender skirt on this example was a dealership display piece that held single-sheet fliers on the new motorcycle.

1955 Model B Hummer

In 1955, Harley-Davidson heralded improvements in its next phase of lightweight motorcycle development: "Here it is . . . the NEW HUMMER! Famous Harley-Davidson quality at a NEW, LOW PRICE!"

Engineering increased the engine capacity of the Model ST to 165cc, so this new Hummer re-established the 125cc machine as the company's entry-level motorcycle. The Hummer was less expensive and more fuel efficient than the 165, reportedly returning 100 miles per gallon. To keep prices down, Harley-Davidson deleted the horn, air cleaner, foot pegs, starter pedal rubber, and instruments. Black wheel rims were standard equipment, and the name badge was a decal rather than the chrome emblem used on the rest of the 1955 lineup. While many of the company lightweights of that period were nicknamed "hummers," this was the first model to take that as its official trade name.

This Pepper Red example was one of 1,040 Hummers the company assembled in 1955.

1962 Model AH Topper with Model LA Sidecar

Robert Phillips of Franklin, Pennsylvania, acquired this particular 1962 Model AH Topper in Skyline Blue and Birch White when he was 16 years old. Phillips paid $445 for the scooter. He sold it to the Archives in 2000.

The Topper is the only Harley-Davidson motorcycle ever to start with a rope-pull mechanism. The manual starter rope is located on the floor in front of the seat. Pulling the rope turns over a 9-horsepower, 165cc two-stroke single-cylinder. The rear body is fiberglass with a storage compartment under the seat.

Harley-Davidson introduced the Model AH in 1960 and kept it in production through 1965. The company assembled 599 of these scooters in 1962.

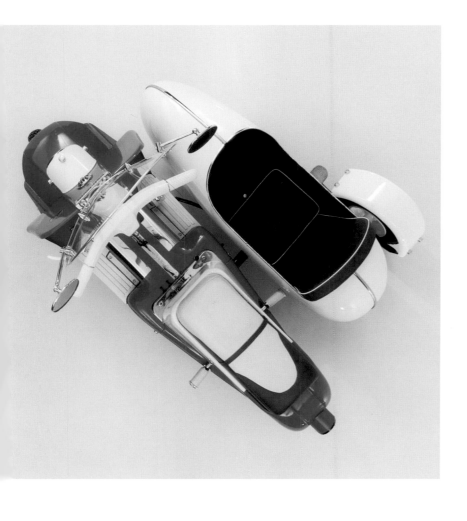

1962 Model AH Topper "Tripoli Shrine"

This scooter was purchased in 1962 for $445 and was used as part of the Tripoli Shrine Motor Corps of Milwaukee, Wisconsin.

The motor scooter sports Shriner logos on each side and on the windshield, a parade flag mounted on the front fender, and a custom-made scooter cover.

The AH models use a variable-speed, Scootaway belt-driven centrifugal transmission that transmits power to a roller-chain final drive. The engine is good for 60 miles per hour and can travel 100 miles on a gallon of gas, giving it impressive range from its 1.7 gallon gas tank.

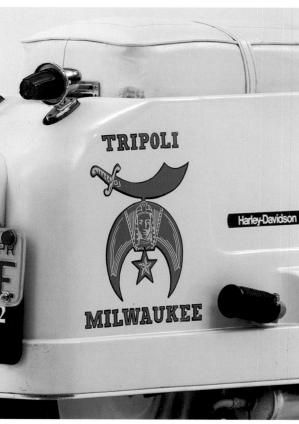

1963 Model BTH Scat

"Off the paved, beaten path . . . through the brush or tall timber . . . your Harley-Davidson Scat is sure-footed as a pack horse, yet lively as a colt. You get way back in there fast where upland or big game is waiting, unmolested by the Public Hunting Grounds' crowds. And you don't have to be an accomplished motorcyclist to ride the trail on a Scat. You'll be surprised how quickly you can learn. Your Harley-Davidson dealer is ready to shown you. Hunt him up in the Yellow Pages."

—Harley-Davidson advertisement

In 1963, Harley-Davidson's advertising for the off-road H version of the company's 175cc Scat targeted buyers outside the company's traditional motorcycle-enthusiast customer base, focusing on the needs of outdoor sportsmen.

The company introduced the BT series in 1960. The original BT used a hard-tail rear frame that did not incorporate any form of suspension control, but in 1963, Harley-Davidson significantly improved these lightweights with the introduction of the concealed "Glide-Ride" rear suspension, a first for the company's smallest machines.

The air cleaner was standard equipment, as was a shortened chrome handlebar, "bobtail" rear fender, and high front fender. BTH Scats rode on 3.5x18 Goodyear Grasshopper tires. Wheelbase was 52 inches, and overall length was 81 inches. It weighed 220 pounds, and its fuel tank held 1.9 gallons.

This black and white Scat sold new for $495. The company produced 877 of these in 1963.

1966 Model BTH Bobcat

"The smooth riding, neatly styled BOBCAT is the all-purpose lightweight. It's great for work . . . great for school . . . great for play. BOBCAT features large headlight and taillight for safe night driving. Big five-inch brakes front and rear stop you fast, safe, and sure. Large new saddle offers more comfort. Newly styled handlebars add to BOBCAT'S easy handling characteristics. Modern 175cc engine offers a world of economy—ride for pennies a day. For a bonus bargain buy—new BOBCAT'S your best bet!"

—Harley-Davidson advertisement

Willie G. Davidson designed the Model BTH Bobcat as one of his first design projects for the company. His one-piece molded-resin body covered the gas tank and rear fender and incorporated a new buddy saddle. He later described it as his attempt to "maximize the visual look of the bike with minimal tooling."

The 175cc engines had aluminum cylinder heads and cases and used mega-phone-style chrome exhaust and drum brakes—this example had optional chrome wheels. The company also offered an optional trail kit. This Indigo Metallic example, one of 1,150 that the company assembled in 1966, had 395 miles on the odometer when it joined the Archives collection. It sold new for $515.

AERMACCHI

**MOTOR
HARLEY-DAVIDSON
CYCLES**

Ala Bianca 175 cc.
105 Km. h

Ala Azzurra 250 cc.
125 Km. h

Chimera 250 cc.
120 Km. h

Wisconsin 250 cc.
130 Km. h

AERMACCHI HARLEY-DAVIDSON

Ala Rossa 175 cc.
130 Km. h

Ala Verde 250 cc.
140 Km. h

Ala d'Oro 175 cc.
155 Km. h
250 cc. 170 Km. h

Ala d'Oro 250 cc. S.
190 Km. h

**AERMACCHI
MOTOR
HARLEY-DAVIDSON
CYCLES**

da un binomio famoso le moto di alta qualità

**AERMACCHI
MOTOR
HARLEY-DAVIDSON
CYCLES**

11

"Funsville, U.S.A."

Italian Lightweights: 1961–1976

By the time the swell of children born in postwar America grew old enough to ride motorcycles, Harley-Davidson was encountering increased competition for their business. The lightweight motorcycles from the Japanese manufacturers gained in popularity by offering features such as direct oil injection and electric starters, features not offered on Harley's aging two-stroke motorcycles.

But the Motor Company had a solution—import the sophisticated lightweights produced by its Italian partner Aermacchi. Aermacchi, an Italian manufacturer founded in 1912, had been producing motorcycles since 1951. In 1960, the Harley-Davidson Motor Company purchased 49 percent of Aermacchi, and Aermacchi retained 49 percent of ownership. (Lockheed Aircraft owned the remaining 2 percent.) The partnership between Harley-Davidson and Aermacchi produced some of the most desirable lightweight motorcycles of the era, along with championship-winning racing motorcycles.

1961 Model C Sprint

"Have your cake and eat it too. Sprint moves you with spirit. Extra punch, stamina, and maneuverability make it an ideal sport machine. Sprint stands for style. This lean, clean-lined beauty commands attention wherever it goes. Daring! Distinctive! The Sprint is a joy to behold . . . a joy to be on! Smartly styled in Calypso Red and White, this slim and trim beauty takes you out of the ordinary . . . takes you into a new world of motorcycling pleasure. For that extra dash—ride a Harley-Davidson Sprint!"

—Harley-Davidson advertisement

The 1961 Model C Sprint was the first product imported under marketing, manufacturing, and distribution agreements between Harley-Davidson and Aermacchi. A horizontal 250cc (15-cubic-inch) four-stroke single-cylinder engine powered this lightweight. The pushrod-actuated engine featured an aluminum-alloy cylinder head and piston, had a 9:1 compression ratio, and developed 18 horsepower at 7,500 rpm. The Sprint delivered 70 miles per gallon and came equipped with a 4-gallon gas tank. The transmission was a four-speed, and the transmission case used a left-side kick starter. The kickstand was on the right side.

1967 Model H Sprint

"H stands for hot, and Sprint H for '67 has got it. Plenty of go . . . plenty of show, plus many new refinements. Small wonder Sprint H has been America's favorite 250 since 1962."

—Harley-Davidson advertisement

In 1967, Aermacchi redesigned the aluminum cylinder and head of its 250cc four-stroke overhead-valve engine, leading to an 18 percent horsepower increase in the Model H Sprint. The H Sprint also got a new, quieter muffler, a new taillight, and a 5.1-gallon road-racer-style gas tank. It weighed 273 pounds. Records indicate Aermacchi–Harley-Davidson produced approximately 2,000 of the Model H Sprints in 1967.

1968 Model ML Rapido

"Meet the Rapido, Harley-Davidson's surprise package of the year. It's 125cc's of pure excitement on a lightweight frame. And you're on top of the action all the way with the new four-speed foot-shift transmission. Add bold new styling and Harley-Davidson's legendary craftsmanship and you've got nothing in front of you but the open road. Come alive in a hurry. Your Rapido 125 is ready and waiting."

—Harley-Davidson advertisement

Harley-Davidson stressed performance in its advertising for its new Model ML Rapido in 1968, though an even more elemental attribute of the machine was its simplicity. The electrical system provided only headlight and taillight illumination, and it used a magneto for ignition spark. This motorcycle weighed 173 pounds and rode on a 46-inch wheelbase.

Aermacchi–Harley-Davidson fabricated roughly 5,000 ML Rapidos for the 1968 model year. This black and silver example sold new for $395.

1968 Model ML Rapido Baja Prototype

Jack Krizman of Kesco, California, extensively modified this particular motorcycle to create the prototype for the subsequent production 1970 MSR-100 Baja model. This prototype used Metzeler knobby tires, and Krizman cross-braced the handlebars, added an ice-racing front fender, cut off the rear fender, and fitted a Filtron air filter and a high exhaust pipe as well as a trail sprocket. He replaced the front fork, rear shocks, seat, and luggage rack and removed the instruments. Archives acquired Krizman's black and orange prototype in 2002.

Baja wins in wild country.

100cc Baja. Wasteland bred for a single purpose. To rough it. With the hottest 2-stroke single that ever hauled past a heavy sled in a sandwash. Ceriani fork and shocks. Malleable, adjustable, quick-change levers. 5-speed gearbox. 11.7-inch clearance. Steel rims. Knobby tires; 21-inch front, 18-inch rear. And stamina. Enough to make a mountain goat blush. Baja. One of the new breed of outperformers. From Harley-Davidson. Number one where it counts . . . off the road and in the records. AMF | HARLEY-DAVIDSON, Milwaukee, Wisconsin 53201.

 the Harley-Davidson outperformers

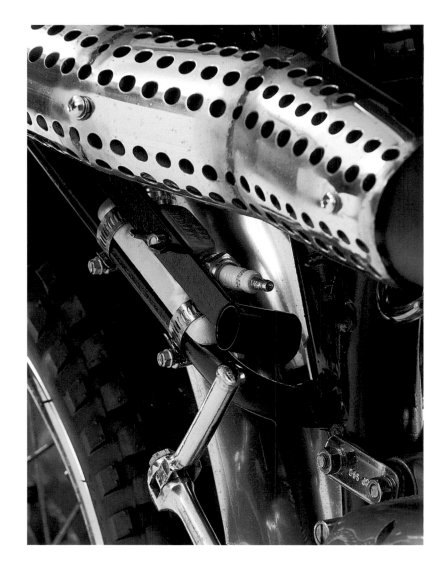

1972 Model MC-65 Shortster

"Shortster . . . The mini-cycle that's mighty like a motorcycle. Shortster's the little guy in the Harley-Davidson family. But its resemblance to our big machines tells you where it comes from . . . and where it belongs. It has mini-motocross forks up front and hydraulic shocks back aft to give you a backwoods ride like no other mini-bike you ever rode. A tough 65cc two-stroke engine cranks out a bag of stump pullin' power. And puts it all on the ground through a three-speed foot-shift. Shortster has full-sized levers and grips . . . just like the big guys. And a wide, comfortable seat that lets you hang in there all day long. Cut loose and head for the good country."

—Harley-Davidson advertisement

Aermacchi–Harley-Davidson produced the little Model MC-65 Shortster in 1972 using the same engine fit in the larger "Leggero" model. The Shortster utilized a large tube-backbone frame and incorporated hydraulic suspension front and rear. It had full lighting, a speedometer, and cross-braced handlebars. The compact lightweight came equipped with a two-up seat, upswept exhaust with a chrome heat shield, and stainless-steel fenders. Tires were 3x10s, and the wheelbase measured 39.2 inches. At 126 pounds, it was the Motor Company's smallest motorcycle and its first minibike. Model year 1972 was the only year this machine was called the Shortster and the only year it used a 65cc engine. For 1973, it featured a 90cc engine with a four-speed transmission and was renamed the X-90.

The partnership manufactured approximately 8,000 of these machines, and this example, in Furious Yellow, sold new for $295.

1976 Model SX-175

"The SX-175, and its brother the SS-175, look much like the high-spirited 250s, but are a bit more subdued, a little more genteel. The 175s are no slouches, however, in the performance department. MOTORCYCLIST Magazine tested one awhile ago and called it 'a giant in the 175 class' and 'a full-blown winner.' CYCLE RIDER called the SX-175 the 'best of all the 175 street/trailers' and added it 'pulls like the proverbial freight train.' What else needs to be said?"

—Harley-Davidson advertisement

Aermacchi's 175cc two-stroke oil-injected single, coupled to a wide-ratio, five-speed transmission, powered Harley-Davidson's 1976 Model SX-175. These engines had chrome-bore aluminum cylinders, capacitive-discharge ignition systems (CDI), and rubber noise dampers on the cylinder fin. These dual-purpose bikes came equipped with cross-braced handlebars, speedometers, tachometers, International Six Day Trials (ISDT) quick-change rear hubs, serrated metal foot pegs, high front fenders, upswept exhaust with heat shields, five-position rear shock absorbers, and directional signals.

Former Motor Company president John A. Davidson rode and enjoyed this motorcycle before he donated it to Archives. Davidson's grandfather was company co-founder William A. Davidson.

12

"The Great American Freedom Machine"

The AMF Era: 1968–1980

Freedom was the theme of the late 1960s, and nothing exemplified freedom like a big, powerful V-twin motorcycle. The image of the iconoclastic motorcyclist aboard his or her Harley-Davidson became ingrained in television, film, and music.

The motorcycles developed by Harley-Davidson during this period reflected that image of freedom. This was a period that saw the Motor Company give birth to the factory custom motorcycle with the advent of the Super Glide in 1971. This would be followed by a series of increasingly radical customs, like the Low Rider and the Wide Glide. In many ways it was a difficult era, one that saw an eroding market share and increasing competition from Japan, but the innovative products developed during this period would ultimately lead to Harley-Davidson regaining its position as the world's preeminent builder of heavyweight motorcycles.

1968 Model FLHFB Electra Glide

Harley-Davidson owned the heavyweight touring bike market when it built this FLHFB Electra Glide for the 1968 model year, and the King of the Highway Group option fitted to this example was aptly named. Powered by a 74-cubic-inch, over-head-valve Shovelhead engine coupled to a four-speed transmission, the Electra Glide represented the pinnacle of touring-bike technology at the time. "The Electra Glide's suspension provides the smoothest ride in the industry," factory literature proclaimed, "and the dual saddle is a classic of touring comfort."

In addition to the King of the Highway Group, this motorcycle features the Chrome Finish Group, which included front and rear chrome safety guards, luggage rack, windshield, passing lamps, and many other pieces. This bike had 5,254 miles on the odometer when Archives acquired it. The factory assembled 5,300 FLH models in 1968. This example, in Jet Fire Orange and Black Wrinkle, sold new for $1,800.

1971 Model FX Super Glide

"Super Glide FX. Call it the Night Train . . . Ultimate superbike. The action-eager muscle machine that says move out! 74-inch engine for blinding performance. Big-inch power with Sportster-like styling . . . One look tells you . . . you're the man for this hot new muscle machine."

—Harley-Davidson advertisement

The motorcycle market experienced dramatic changes in the late 1960s and early 1970s as the baby boom generation came of age and began buying motorcycles by the millions. Young people were more interested in the customized motorcycles shown in films like *Easy Rider* than they were in the luxurious touring bikes that Harley-Davidson built, and these new buyers demanded a new style of motorcycle. With limited financial resources to develop a new line of motorcycles, Chief Designer Willie G. Davidson mated a Big Twin chassis and running gear with a Sportster front end to create the 1971 FX Super Glide. He removed the rubber fork boots (but only for the first year of production), added a one-piece tapered fiberglass seat/fender combination (referred to as the boat-tail), and created a lean factory custom. It was offered with kick start only.

This example is painted in what the Motor Company calls "Sparkling America"—white, with red, blue, and white Mylar panels on the fenders and tanks. The factory assembled 4,700 FX models in 1971, and this version sold for $2,230.

the Harley-Davidson
Outperformers

1973 Model FLH-1200 Electra Glide: The Rhinestone Harley-Davidson

Margaret and Russ Townsend of Northampton, Pennsylvania, purchased this Electra Glide new in May 1973. Both of them rode it regularly, but during an extended recuperation period after an accident, when Russ was unable to ride, he began to decorate the motorcycle. Ultimately, he placed $3,000 worth of red, white, and blue rhinestones on the motorcycle, along with more than two hundred lights. Russ and Margaret also equipped the motorcycle with a frame-mounted seat, an aftermarket Tour Pack, a citizens band radio, an S&S carburetor, and several homemade light bars and other pieces of

trim. The motorcycle had a cast front wheel and a laced rear wheel.

Electra Glides were powered by 74-cubic-inch Shovelhead engines mated to four-speed transmissions. These models received new rectangular rear swing-arms and rocker cutoff switches in 1973. Wheelbase was 61.5 inches, and in stock trim they weighed 722 pounds, though estimates place this one at well over 800 pounds. The Archives acquired this otherwise black and white—but now truly unique—motorcycle in April 2000 from Schloch's Harley-Davidson in Stroudsburg, Pennsylvania,

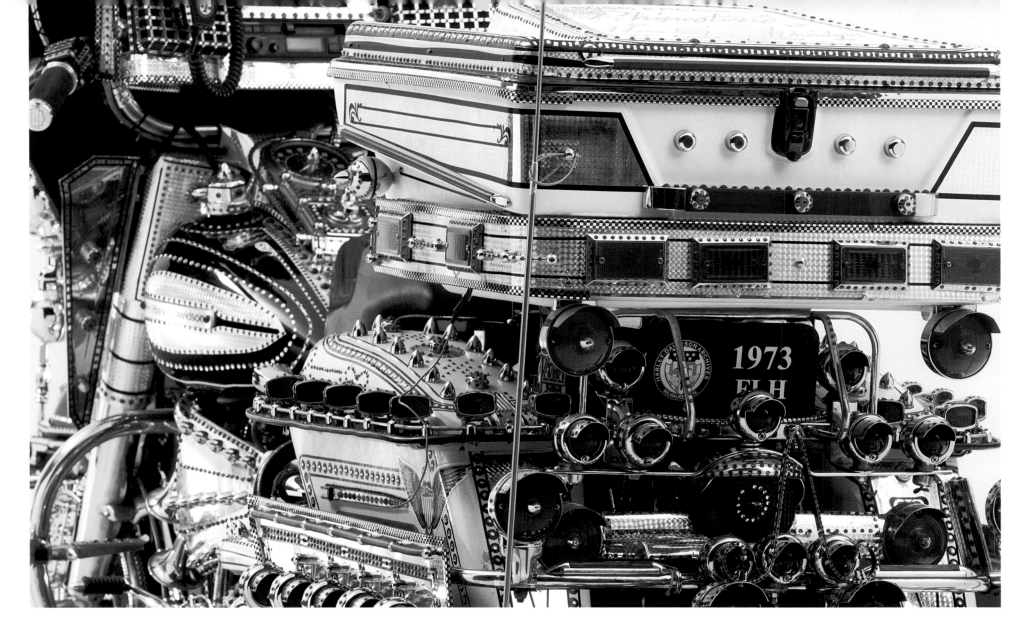

1973 Model XL-1000

According to records, this 1973 XL-1000 was among the last bikes to be assembled in Milwaukee, during March and April 1973, before XL production moved to new facilities in York, Pennsylvania.

The year 1973 marked the beginning of a temporary hiatus for the Sportster name. That year Harley-Davidson dropped model names, so the model previously called the XLH Sportster became the XL-1000 (the electric-start version) and the XLCH (the kick-start version). This was one of 9,875 XL-1000s manufactured in 1973.

Harley-Davidson Motor Company President John A. Davidson owned and rode this motorcycle. Davidson was a grandson of company co-founder William A. Davidson. When he gifted this Sunburst Blue motorcycle to Archives, it had 3,483 miles on the odometer.

Carve your name on blacktop.

The Harley-Davidson XLCH-1000.

With 1000cc's of gut power that wins respect wherever it goes.

All new front forks, hydraulic front disc brake and adjustable shocks make sure you enjoy the going. (Electric start on XL-1000).

Take on any two-lane blacktop and leave your name on the asphalt.

Or blow the doors off the big bores at the strip.

But regardless of which way you like your riding, you've got the power.

It's up to you to earn the glory.

Harley-Davidson,
Milwaukee, Wisconsin 53201
Member Motorcycle Industry Council

AMF
Harley-Davidson

Harley-Davidson XLCH-1000.
The Great American Freedom Machine.

1974 Model Y-440 Snowmobile

"Your first Harley-Davidson—a snowmobile built with a difference," an advertisement for Harley-Davidson's first 440cc snowmobile touted in 1974. "Style that stops your mind. Hot lines, hot performance."

Harley-Davidson had entered the burgeoning snowmobile market in 1972 with a machine powered by a 398cc parallel-twin two-stroke engine. A belt-driven, centrifugal-clutch, automatic transmission delivered power to an 18-inch-wide track attached to either a bogie-wheel rear suspension (as on this example) or an available slide-rail system. The machine was equipped with both manual and electric starters, a solid-state 12-volt system with capacitive-discharge ignition (CDI), and dual-sealed beam headlights. It had a foam-insulated cowl, console, and acoustical intake for quieter operation. It had a 6.2-gallon gas tank. Adjustable handlebars and a steering dampener directed the shock-dampened chrome skis.

You'll never forget your first Harley-Davidson.

Neither will we.

Your first Harley-Davidson—a snowmobile built with a difference. Style that stops your mind. Hot lines, hot performance. An all-new 398cc 2-stroke twin; designed, developed and manufactured by Harley-Davidson.

There's another Harley-Davidson difference, one that can be even more important to you. Most manufacturers started with a machine, and then went looking for dealers. Harley-Davidson began looking for dealers in 1903.

Harley-Davidson owners will never be left out in the cold. We build a quality machine. And put our name and years of experience in recreational vehicles solidly behind it. Trained, qualified dealers. Service and parts, locally available. In snowmobiles—as in motorcycles — Harley-Davidson means performance today. And service tomorrow. AMF | Harley-Davidson, Milwaukee, Wis. 53201.

it's the year of the Harley-Davidson difference.

1975 Model OHC-1100 Experimental

Harley-Davidson built this motorcycle in the early 1970s as part of the experimental V-1100 project. This particular vehicle was the styling study (some of this model's engine components are made of wood), but Archives does have prototype and test engines that ran on test stands. The engine shown here represented an 1100cc overhead-camshaft engine with offset cylinders to promote better rear-cylinder cooling. It is unknown whether the unitized transmission would have been a four- or five-speed unit.

Engineering designed a triangulated frame for this motorcycle with rubber mounts to isolate the drivetrain. It was equipped with dual front disc brakes, directional signal lights, dual carburetors, vertical rear shock absorbers, and a tachometer and speedometer. It had an unusual exhaust system with twin pipes that emerged from the front cylinder and traveled down each side of the frame to a collector under the swing arm, then emerged into dual mufflers. The rear cylinder had a single exhaust pipe that connected to the transverse crossover. The motorcycle was never produced and no sale price ever was developed.

1975 Model FLH-1200

Though Harley-Davidson had begun to experience fierce competition from Japanese manufacturers by 1975, its FLH still dominated the heavyweight luxury touring bike market. Other manufacturers were offering motorcycles in the 1000cc-plus range, but none offered the touring amenities of the FLH. This example is equipped with a front engine guard, passing lamps, chrome luggage rack, saddlebags, hazard warning flashers, and cast wheels mounted with 5.1x16 dual whitewall tires. It has 10-inch disc brakes front and rear. Records indicate the factory assembled 7,400 FLH models in 1975.

1976 Model FLH-1200 Liberty Edition

For 1976, Harley-Davidson assembled the limited-production Liberty Edition to commemorate the U.S. Bicentennial. It features the "Sequin Metallic Black" paint shown here, which suspends aluminum chips in clear acrylic. It has multi-colored decals on the tank and fairing, which marked the first re-use of the bar and shield logo in modern Harley-Davidson history. It also marked the adoption of the eagle as an unofficial corporate mascot. Equipped with the Super Deluxe Buddy Seat, double-stripe whitewall tires, and passing lamps, this motorcycle also features Tour Pak luggage and gold-colored tank nameplates. The factory assembled a total of 11,891 FLH models throughout 1976, although there is no exact record of Liberty Edition production. The original price was $3,995.

1976 Model XLCH-1000

When Harley-Davidson designed the XL series of motorcycles (and the K series that preceded it) in the 1950s, engineering had given the new middleweight sporting bikes foot shifters on the right side of the engine cases, since there was no standard location for shifters at that time. New federal regulations for the U.S. market for 1975 standardized the location of the shifter on the left side of the motorcycle, which meant moving the location of the shifter on XL models. (Big Twins already featured shifters on the left side of the cases.) Because the

Motor Company had not completed engineering and tooling in time to introduce a true left-side shifter, 1975–1976 XL models used a long linkage from the right side of the motorcycle to the left to relocate the shifter.

This Vivid Brown XLCH, which features the new-for-1976 4-inch-thick "Hi-Lo" seat, had 11,792 miles on the odometer when Archives acquired it in 1995. It is one of 5,238 XLCH models produced in 1976.

1977 Model FXS-1200 Low Rider

The Motor Company's ad copy resorted to poetry when it introduced Harley-Davidson's newest motorcycle: "One Mean Machine . . . 1977 . . . Year of the lowdown, mighty and mean!" The Low Rider, with its extended fork, drag bar on 3.5-inch risers, cast wheels, black and silver engine with painted side covers, and oil cooler, took the concept of the factory custom motorcycle to a level previously unimagined. Engineering specified dual front disc brakes and a 10-inch rear disc. The Low Rider has highway pegs, a "Fat Bob" 3.5-gallon gas tank with an instrument cluster, two-into-one collector exhaust, white-lettered tires, and 1917-style tank graphics.

The FXS is equipped with both an electric starter and kick starter, and it boasts a seat height of just 27 inches. It weighs 607 pounds. The factory produced 3,742 FXS models in 1977.

1977 Model XLCR-1000 Café Racer

Willie G. Davidson conceived and designed the XLCR-1000 Café Racer, and Milwaukee-area fabricator Jim Haubert assembled the original prototype. That first example used a flat-sided gas tank inspired by the XR-750 racing tank. During testing, issues with tank welds related to gas welding procedures cropped up. These were exacerbated by the length of the required welds, but preheating the seams before welding took place solved the problems. Knee indentations pressed into the tank also made the sides more rigid.

The production version of the bike, which uses Harley-Davidson's 1000cc Sportster engine with an integral four-speed transmission, incorporates a small,

handlebar-mounted fairing, drag bars, a solo seat on a racing-type fiberglass fender, cast wheels front and rear, and dual disc brakes up front with a single disc on the rear.

The XLCR introduced an entirely new triangulated frame that the company later used on the 1979 Sportster. Decoration on the bike includes die-stamped bar and shield tank emblems.

Each of the production XLCR models received a 100 percent audit and was run on the test track at the factory at York, Pennsylvania, to ensure quality and performance standards. York manufactured 1,923 XLCR models in 1977.

ONLY ONE MAN COULD HAVE DONE THIS.

Harley-Davidson's new Cafe Racer couldn't have been built by a committee. There's no compromise.

Only one man could have built the Cafe Racer. Willie G. If he wore a suit, he'd be William G. Davidson. But he doesn't. So he's Willie G., the man who designed the Super Glide, and now, the all-new, 1977 XLCR Cafe Racer.

"I wanted to build the ultimate, no compromise bike. So I built it first, then presented it. Before the presentation, I said to myself, 'If they like it, we're going to build it. If they don't, I'll keep it for myself.'"

They liked it.

No wonder. A street legal Cafe Racer in black on black, Willie G.'s creation may be the ultimate customizing job:

He took the engine from the powerful 1977 Sportster. Sculpted the seat and rear end to resemble the famous XR-750 racer. Added a specially-designed gas tank. Put on a unique Siamese exhaust system with all black pipes.

Those pipes, coupled with the Sportster engine, make the Cafe Racer the most powerful production cycle Harley-Davidson has ever built.

Possessed with an ability to compete with the best of Europe's Cafe Racers, it can hustle down a twisting road while providing outstanding handling at high speeds.

And every detail, from the mating of aluminum cast wheels with Goodyear Eagle AT tires, to the positioning of the footpegs and the inclusion of low-profile handlebars, the careful selection of Willie G.

You'll find dual front discs matched with a single disc brake in the rear. A blunted, snub-nose, black fairing with a smoke-colored

windshield. And everywhere there's black. Black trim, black cases, black horn, air cleaner cover and pipes.

Even the reproduction of the antique Harley-Davidson brass plate on the gas tank comes from the same source. "Why did I go to the old plate? I just like it."

Willie G. built himself a Cafe Racer. Now you can buy it. However, there will only be a limited number available. See your Harley-Davidson dealer for details.

Until you've been on a Harley-Davidson, you haven't been on a motorcycle.

We believe in safety first. Before you start out, light your lights, put on your helmet and watch out for the other guy. Follow owner's manual for maintenance.

1978 Model XLH-1000 Sportster 75th Anniversary

In 1978, Harley-Davidson celebrated its 75th anniversary by advertising historical facts that illustrated its growth: In 1903, its only factory measured 10x15 feet, 150 square feet. By 1978, Harley-Davidson had four plants and occupied 1.2 million square feet—roughly 275 acres—of manufacturing floor space. In 1903 and 1904, William Harley and Arthur Davidson assembled three motorcycles. In 1978, 3,400 employees designed, tested, assembled, and delivered 48,000 individual vehicles, including 3 families of motorcycles and 19 model lines.

The company also offered Anniversary editions of its motorcycles, like this XLH-1000 Sportster (after a brief hiatus the Sportster name had returned to the lineup). The Anniversary model features special gold pinstriping on the fenders and gold-colored cast wheels with nine spokes. The factory manufactured 2,323 XLH-1000 Sportster Anniversary editions in 1978.

1978 Model FLHS-1200 Electra Glide Sport

"The wide-tracked wonder built to obey your wanderlust . . . Strength. Stamina . . . 1200 cc's of motorized magnificence. Just for the fun of it. For you. Take on the highway. Mile after mile after mile . . . The Great American Freedom Machine."

—Harley-Davidson advertisement

The Motor Company introduced the FLHS model late in the 1978 model year. It incorporated a single exhaust, laced wheels, and a three-dimensional nameplate on its 5-gallon gas tank. It had a frame-mounted step seat, electric starter, and double-stripe sidewall tires. It had no windshield, saddlebags, or fairing. Tires were 5.1x16s, and wheelbase was 61 inches. There are no illustrations or descriptions of this vehicle in any company marketing or sales literature, and the number of FLHS models produced and its sale price were not recorded.

1979 Model XL-1000

In 1979, Harley-Davidson gave the XL-1000 Sportster the triangulated XLCR frame, which replaced the same basic frame that had been in use since the introduction of the K-series in 1952. Engineering and design concealed the battery and oil tank behind side covers. The 1000cc engine had a new "Ham Can" air cleaner that increased air flow by 10 percent, and it used a Siamese exhaust configuration that increased torque and midrange horsepower. This was the first year for XL-series solid-state ignition. Designers carried over the Anniversary edition's nine-spoke cast wheels without the gold anodizing. The company assembled 6,525 of these XLs in 1979. This Brilliant Red example sold new for $3,610. When Archives acquired it in 1979, the motorcycle had 11,267 miles on the odometer.

Harley-Davidson Sportster.

THE DREAM OF EVERY RED-BLOODED AMERICAN.

HARLEY-DAVIDSON HAS NEVER FORGOTTEN THE BASIC RELATIONSHIP BETWEEN MAN AND MOTORCYCLE.

From the start, when you're first aware of that incredible V-Twin rhythm and the classic styling that nobody's ever been able to duplicate, you realize the Sportster® represents the big leap. Make it, and you're no longer Everyman. You're Somebody.

Get in behind our new buckhorn handlebars, grab on and take a look at what you've got going for you. From a strong, durable frame through an explosive, highly efficient performance package, this is a motor-cycle that exhibits the soul of Harley-Davidson. Unquestionably, the best handling, best perform-ing Sportster we've ever put together.

In an age where others fight to hold onto whatever performance level they once achieved, Harley-Davidson, through the addition of twin-chromed, siamese exhausts, optimizes horse-power and actually increases the torque exploding from the 1000cc, V-Twin powerplant.

V-Fire™ solid state ignition gives you quick, sure starts, and is virtually maintenance free. While a high-flow air cleaner allows more air to reach the carburetor, helping the engine breathe free and easy.

The oil tank and battery are tucked away under the frame, so the motorcycle sits lean and narrow, and you sit a lot more comfortably. Three stainless steel disc brakes (two in front, one in the rear) provide the stopping muscle. And the wheels are 9-spoke cast aluminum.

As always, you'll be able to add your own personalized touch to your Sportster, as Harley-Davidson once again offers the widest variety of accessories in the industry.

If you've never been on a Harley-Davidson, the Sportster is one motorcycle that will give you an eye-opening lesson: namely, that dreams can become reality. All it takes is the guts to quit dreaming and start moving to your Harley-Davidson dealer.

AMF
Harley-Davidson

UNTIL YOU'VE BEEN ON A HARLEY-DAVIDSON, YOU HAVEN'T BEEN ON A MOTORCYCLE.

We support the Motorcycle Safety Foundation and the A.M.A. and believe in safety first. Always ride with lights and helmet. Help keep insurance costs down. lock your bike. Follow owners manual for maintenance. Specifications subject to change without notice.

1980 Model FXB-80 Sturgis

"Out of the Badlands comes one mean custom. Introducing the Twin-Belt Drive Sturgis. In the heat of the year, out in the buzzard country of South Dakota, these badlands come to life. The little town of Sturgis starts to rumble and shake under the weight of thousands upon thousands of Harley V-Twins. They come from Oakland and Long Island and just about every place in between. They come to swap stories and admire the scoots that got them there. They come because they all have one thing in common: Motorcycles. Harley-Davidson Motorcycles."

—Harley-Davidson advertisement

Powered by an 80-cubic-inch engine with a four-speed transmission, the 1980 FXB-80 Sturgis was the first modern belt-drive Harley-Davidson, and it used belts instead of chains in both the primary and secondary drives. About the belt, the ad copy says: "It's lighter and simpler than a shaft. It doesn't eat up horsepower like a shaft. Compared to a chain, it's smoother shifting, quieter, requires no lube and needs minimal adjustment." The company assembled 1,470 of these striking bikes in 1980.

OUT OF THE BADLANDS COMES ONE MEAN CUSTOM.   INTRODUCING THE TWIN-BELT DRIVE STURGIS.

In the heat of the year, out in the buzzard country of South Dakota, those badlands come to life. The little town of Sturgis starts to rumble and shake under the weight of thousands upon thousands of Harley V-Twins. They come from Oakland and Long Island and just about every place in between. They come to swap stories and admire the scoots that got them there. They come because they all have one thing in common. Motorcycles. Harley-Davidson Motorcycles.

Out of this phenomenon the new custom Sturgis was born. Black as the hills around dusk, with just a hint of orange to make it a whole lot of Harley. 80 cubic inches of stamping steel with two factory firsts to set it up on a whole new plateau.

Sturgis is the first production bike with twin belt drive. It's lighter and simpler than a shaft. It doesn't eat up the horsepower like a shaft. Compared to a chain, it's smoother shifting, quieter, requires no lube and needs minimal adjustment.

Sturgis is also the first production belt drive bike with a compensating sprocket on the primary drive to give you remarkably smooth power flow.

To fire up this big black on black on black stallion, put your boot to the kick start or your thumb to the button. Our new V-Fire II® digital electronic ignition system is the hottest, simplest, most efficient one we've ever put into a bike. The massive 80 V-Twin speaks for itself.

That's the technical side of it. Out in the real world it means you can chuck it all, strap on your chaps and head for the hills. Just sit back, grab the drag style bars on the 3½" risers, kick your feet up on the highway pegs, check the gauges on the Fat Bob tank, and dodge tumbleweeds all day long. With the extended forks out front, you're riding tall in the saddle just 27" off the ground.

You can only ride the fences so long before you head for that opening and cut loose. You've got to ride to get the cobwebs out. You head for the freedom of your custom bike on the open road. You head for Sturgis or someplace like it.

No, Sturgis is not some weak kneed imitation sled out of a freighter tied up at Long Beach. It's a badlands tested factory custom, from the only company that knows what "custom" really means. It's not just another new machine. It's much more than that. It's a Harley-Davidson.

1980 Model FXWG-80 Wide Glide (ex–Malcolm Forbes)

With its "bobtail" rear fender, forward foot controls, wide 41mm front forks with extended tubes, flamed 5-gallon gas tank (with center instrument panel), and staggered shorty exhausts, the 1980 FXWG-80 Wide Glide came closer to replicating the look of the radical custom chopped motorcycles of the day than had any factory custom yet.

Millionaire capitalist Malcolm Forbes acquired this particular motorcycle as a new vehicle. During his 8,375 miles of riding, he added a rear-mounted flag holder and replaced the factory air-cleaner with a custom S&S unit. Forbes' Wide Glide was one of 6,085 that the company manufactured in 1980. Archives acquired Forbes' motorcycle for the collection after he died in February 1990.

HARLEY-DAVIDSON

13
"Number One"

Modern Racing Bikes: 1965–2006

The late 1960s was a period of dramatic change in American motorcycle racing. Rules dating back to the 1920s had set in stone the formula for building a motorcycle to compete successfully in the American Motorcyclist Association's premier Grand National series, rules that favored 45-cubic-inch side-valve engine configurations. But by the 1960s, every motorcycle and automobile manufacturer doing business in the U.S. market had long since abandoned the antiquated side-valve design, meaning Grand National racers had little or no relation to the production bikes Harley-Davidson sold its customers.

When rule changes inevitably came, the Motor Company struggled to develop a competitive engine using its XL architecture, but after a few years of trial and error, Harley-Davidson's racing engineers developed a bike—the XR-750—that would dominate the Grand National series to this very day, taking on all challengers from Europe and Japan.

1965 Model CRTT Road Racer

"Again No. 1 in The Nation. Number 1 in the nation . . . number 1 in the world. Harley-Davidson's record-shattering accomplishments at Bonneville and on America's race courses during 1964 are conclusive proof of brand superiority. Decisive wins for Harley-Davidson began at Daytona and continued throughout the year. These were great wins . . . sensational wins . . . big wins . . . from coast to coast. Ten national titles in all, to once again put Harley-Davidson in the number 1 spot. Put yourself in the same position . . . ride a winner."

—Harley-Davidson dealer brochure

Harley-Davidson's CRTT Road Racer went through extensive development and refinement between 1961 and 1968. It began as a long-stroke four-speed and ended up a short-stroke five-speed. Its 250cc horizontally mounted, overhead-valve single-cylinder engine began with a 9.5:1 compression ratio and 8,500 rpm redline, good for 22 horsepower. The 1968 version had a 12:1 compression ratio and generated 32 horsepower at 10,400 rpm. Front and rear brakes were 8-inch-diameter drums; the front was a double leading-shoe design. The 1965 model shown here featured a 10.5:1 compression ratio and generated 28 horsepower at 9,500 rpm.

The Italian factory built 35 of these CR models for competition in 1965, although records did not specify how many of them were TT road-racing types. The company sold these motorcycles for $690 in 1966; the price of this 1965 example is unknown, but it would have been slightly less. Archives acquired this motorcycle in 1998. The original owner had rebuilt it from scratch and never started it.

1967 Model CR Dirt Track Racer

The Model CR Dirt Track Racer used a horizontal 250cc overhead-valve, single-cylinder engine that differed from the CRTT Road Racer only slightly. The most substantial difference was that the primary-gear drive ratio was 20 percent higher on the TT version to allow it to reach higher top speeds on paved road courses. Assembled for racing, this particular example had an aftermarket dirt-track racing frame with no rear suspension and no brakes. The bike was equipped with a sprung saddle, number plates, a chrome megaphone exhaust, and an oversize rear sprocket. The racing department produced 50 CR motorcycles in 1967. This red and black example had a racing history when Archives acquired it in 1998.

1970 Model XRTT-750 Road Racer

Earl Widman, Harley-Davidson's St. Louis dealer, assembled this particular motorcycle. He modified a Lowboy KR frame to accommodate the 748cc overhead-valve twin XR engine and four-speed transmission. Widman's son, Ron, raced this motorcycle during the early 1970s. Sometime later, Widman sold the motorcycle to George Schott, the Harley-Davidson dealer in Lewiston, Maine, who competed on it as a drag racer. Eventually, Dan Caulkins of Decatur, Illinois, acquired the bike from Schott, installed a Sportster engine in it, and used it on the street. Finally, he put a correct XR engine in and restored it to the same condition and appearance as when Ron Widman used it in competition.

The Model XRTT-750 Road Racers had aluminum oil tanks, staggered dual exhausts, Smiths tachometers, four leading-shoe front brakes, and rear disc brakes. They raced on aluminum rims with 3x18 front and 3.5x18 rear tires. The racing department gave these machines oversized 6-gallon fiberglass gas tanks, enabling them to compete in the grueling Daytona 200-mile race with fewer pit stops for refueling. Much attention was paid to shielding the rider's left leg from extreme heat when tucked in. Archives acquired this motorcycle in 2004.

1970 Model XR-750 Dirt Track Racer

Harley-Davidson developed the XR-750 Dirt Track Racer in 1970 as a competition motorcycle to fill the gap between the discontinued KR racers and the alloy-engine XR-750 that would appear in 1972. This cast-iron 748cc overhead-valve engine with its integral four-speed transmission was a de-stroked version of the XLR powerplant (the competition version of the XL street engine) developed to meet the new American Motorcyclist Association (AMA) rules for overhead-valve engines. The racing engine used different valves, cylinder heads, pistons, camshafts, and tuned exhausts. The racing department mounted these pieces onto a racing frame and topped it off with a 2.5-gallon fiberglass gas tank and rear fender/seat combination with a foam cushion. The suspension used Ceriani front forks and Girling rear shock absorbers. It had aluminum wheels and raced on 4x19-inch tires. Equipped for competition, the oil reservoir held 3 quarts. The throttle linkage was adjusted to accommodate one quarter turn to open fully.

The 1970 XR-750 was soon followed by the 1972 model, which used aluminum cylinders and heads to address overheating problems and to allow for a higher compression ratio.

Records suggest that the company assembled 200 identical copies of these Jetfire Orange motorcycles in order to meet AMA production class requirements. They sold for $3,200. This particular example had a racing history at the time Archives acquired it in 1998.

1975 Model XR-750 Dirt Track Racer

The engine of the XR-750 featured aluminum cylinders and cylinder heads, dual Mikuni carburetors, tuned dual-reverse cone exhausts, and displaced 750cc. These bikes had four-speed transmissions, Ceriani front forks, and aluminum wheels running 4x19-inch tires in front and back. At the rear, the racing department fitted Girling racing shock absorbers and a fiberglass seat/fender piece. The company sold these bikes without brakes, though rear brakes were required for dirt-track racing. Owners could purchase brakes from the Harley-Davidson factory or add aftermarket brakes from other manufacturers.

Archives acquired this motorcycle in 2002.

1975 Model SX-250 Desert Racer

"Normally Friday the 13th is considered an unlucky day for most, but for the team of Larry Roessler and Bruce Ogilvie, Friday, June 13 was one of their luckiest, for it was on that day the pair rode their Harley-Davidson SX-250 to a class win, an overall motorcycle win, and to second overall vehicle in the punishing event called the Baja 500. The Baja 500 is more than just an off-road race. It is an annual battle among motorcycles, cars, dune buggies, heat, sand, cactus, rocks, stray animals and aching muscles. About the only event tougher is the Baja 1000 scheduled for later in the year."

—Harley-Davidson advertisement

Dale's Modern Cycle of San Bernardino, California, sponsored Larry Roessler and Bruce Ogilvie and did the extensive preparation on the 1975 Model SX-250 Desert Racer that carried the pair to an overall motorcycle victory in the 1975 running of the Baja 500. While the engine already had a chrome-bore aluminum cylinder, Dale's engineers added a tuned expansion chamber, good for a 6-horsepower increase, and a capacitive-discharge ignition. While equipping the bike with plastic fenders and a Vesco 4-gallon tank, Dale's also installed five-position shocks, a long-travel front suspension, and cross-braced handlebars. They moved the shock mounts 1 inch forward and replaced the front fork with a Boge-Mulholland unit with 7.5 inches of travel. They angled the steering head out 3 degrees, lengthened the rear swingarm 1 inch, and heavily reinforced the frame.

The race route, from Ensenada, Mexico, through the desert, over mountains, and along the shoreline and back to Ensenada, covered 390 miles. Roessler and Ogilvie started 30th out of 375 entrants and, excluding a mandatory midway-point 30-minute layover, they completed the course in 8 hours, 16 minutes, 53 seconds.

The factory assembled 11,000 SX-250 models for 1975. This orange race winner was the most significant.

1977 XR-750 Racer "Cutaway"

The racing department originally built this cutaway engine for engineering use in the development of the XR-750. When they finished with the project, it was made into a display vehicle. Viewing the engine from either side it is possible to see into the 750cc overhead-valve aluminum cylinders, four-speed transmission, and 36mm Mikuni carburetors. The primary and cam case covers were cut open as well. This Jetfire Orange example combines a 1972 engine with a 1980 frame. While production XR-750 models used Ceriani front forks, this Archives example has a Marzocchi fork instead. For display purposes, engineering installed new valves, pistons, rods, flywheel assembly, camshaft, magneto, and carburetors with their paper air filters. The company built 200 examples of the XR-750 to meet AMA racing production class regulations in 1972.

1978 Model DT-250 Short Track Racer

This orange 1978 DT-250 Short Track Racer was a factory team bike, and the number "1" plate suggests that team member Scott Parker may have competed on this motorcycle. Within its Champion chromium-molybdenum frame sits a 250cc two-stroke single-cylinder engine with a five-speed transmission. This racer has a swing-arm rear suspension, rear disc brake, and compression release used by the rider to slow the vehicle as he or she entered turns (making a unique sound in the process). The left foot peg is set back for dirt-track racing. Harley-Davidson sold the DT-250 engine to recognized racers in the early 1980s, and these competitors put the engines and transmissions into their own frames.

1989 Model XR-750 Hillclimb Racer

Lou Gerencer Sr., an Elkhart, Indiana, Harley-Davidson dealer and national hillclimb champion, campaigned this 1989 XR-750. The extended frame and rear swing-arm kept the majority of the vehicle's weight as far forward as possible to keep the vehicle from flipping over backwards when climbing steep hills. Gerencer added mechanical fuel injection to the engine, which runs on nitro methane and produces in excess of 150 horsepower. Obviously this modified engine has a very short and violent lifespan between rebuilds, but it enabled Gerencer to earn the Number 1 plate seen on the bike. Archives acquired this racer from Gerencer in 2002.

1990 Double-Engine Dragster

Chrome Horse Racing of Spencer, Iowa, and racer Gary "Tater" Gilmore fabricated this dragster in 1990 using two Evolution engines with Delkron cases and HyPerformance heads. Chrome Horse built the machine with an open primary drive, a wide slick on the rear, and a road-racing tire on the front. They installed a dual-coil ignition on each engine and used nitrous-oxide injection. The motorcycle has dual steering dampers, an air-adjustable front fork, and a wheelie bar.

Records indicate that this was the first Harley-Davidson to run the quarter-mile in less than 8.0 seconds elapsed time. Archives acquired this motorcycle in 1994.

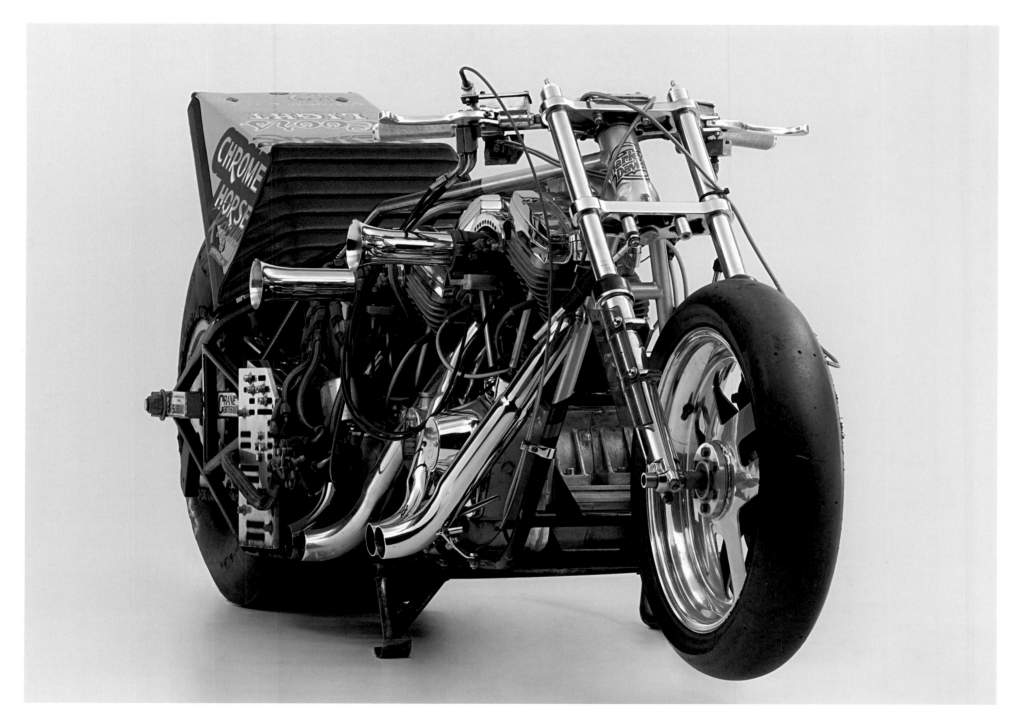

1994 Model VR-1000 Road Racer

In 1994, Harley-Davidson manufactured 50 VR-1000 models, the minimum number needed to satisfy AMA homologation regulations for the Superbikes class. These motorcycles used a 60-degree 1000cc overhead cam, water-cooled, offset V-twin engine with six-speed transmission. When first produced in 1994, the VR-1000 generated 135 horsepower and redlined at 10,000 rpm. In 2001, in its final form as shown here, the engine produced 160 horsepower at more than 11,000 rpm, thanks in part to its electronic fuel-injection system.

This orange and black racer originally was the backup motorcycle for team member Michael Smith, who replaced Scott Russell as Pascal Picotte's teammate for the final season. Once Harley-Davidson withdrew from Superbike racing after the 2001 season, the company assigned this example to Archives. It was priced at $50,000 in 1994.

1994 Dragster

Harley-Davidson engineer Paul Wiers built and raced this highly modified FL dragster. The 114-cubic-inch engine develops approximately 200 horsepower. Wiers set three world records with this machine. He was the first Harley-Davidson–mounted rider to run an eighth-mile in less than 6 seconds (5.96 seconds at 116.3 miles per hour), and his best quarter-mile time was 9.75 seconds at 138.47 miles per hour.

1995 Model XR-750 Hillclimber

Lou Gerencer Jr., of Elkhart, Indiana, followed in his father's footsteps and won several hillclimb championships on this elongated-frame XR-750. The engine is an aluminum-alloy, 750cc racing powerplant. Gerencer used dual carburetors with fuel injection, an inverted front fork, knobby tires with a rear chain, a flat aluminum rear fender, and a lengthened and boxed rear swing-arm. Archives acquired this racer from the Gerencer family in 2002.

2006 V-Rod Destroyer

"The thunder of wide-open exhaust and a cloud of tire smoke will announce the arrival of the VRXSE Screamin' Eagle V-Rod Destroyer, a 165+hp, professional-level drag-racing motorcycle designed exclusively for competition by Harley-Davidson Custom Vehicle Operations and available to racers through Harley-Davidson dealers."

—www.harley-davidson.com

Harley-Davidson's Custom Vehicle Operations (CVO) program created the Destroyer strictly for competitive drag racing; it was never designed to be a street-legal motorcycle. CVO based the Destroyer on the production V-Rod, but the modification list was so extensive that any resemblance to the street bike was purely superficial. The engine was bored and stroked to 1300cc, with forged, high-compression (14:1) pistons, high-strength ductile-iron cylinder sleeves, and high-flow racing cylinder heads that feature CNC porting, competition valves, springs, seats, and keepers designed to work with high-lift camshafts. An electric-over-air shift system stirred the racing transmission, which transmitted power to the rear wheel via the same chain final drive used on the Screamin' Eagle/Vance and Hines Pro Stock Bike racing motorcycle. Horsepower figures weren't specified, but peak power was reached at 9,700 rpm. The Destroyer required the use of U4 racing gasoline.

REVDDD00299

14

"The Eagle Soars Alone"

Buyback and Beyond: 1981–1989

The early 1980s proved a difficult time to be in the motorcycle manufacturing business. The old manufacturers from Europe were dropping like flies, and the fabled British motorcycle industry ceased to exist. The Japanese manufacturers engaged in business practices that ran afoul of the Federal Trade Commission, making business even more difficult in the U.S. market.

But as dark as the era seemed, visionaries within Harley-Davidson understood that with the right leadership the Motor Company had a brilliant future. For all its missteps, AMF had done many things right, especially when it came to product development, and with the Evolution engine in the pipeline, Harley-Davidson motorcycles would soon be the equal of the very best machines produced in Europe and Japan. With the U.S. government cracking down on the questionable trade practices of the Japanese manufacturers, the timing was perfect for the 13-member buyback team to retake control and guide Harley-Davidson into its most successful and prosperous period yet.

1981 Model FLT-80 Tour Glide

On February 26, 1981, a team of Harley-Davidson's senior executives signed a letter of intent to purchase the Motor Company from AMF. In addition to the company, team members received specially prepared black Tour Glide motorcycles. The company engraved and installed a personalized commemorative timer cover on each bike.

This particular example went to Jeffrey Bleustein, vice president of engineering at the time. He subsequently became president and later chief executive officer.

The FLT uses the company's 80-inch overhead-valve engine and five-speed transmission. For the 1981 model year, engineering revised the engine to operate on unleaded gasoline. This motorcycle has a rubber-mounted drivetrain, a frame-mounted fairing, and an enclosed oil-bath final-drive chain. The "balanced front end" positions the fork behind the steering head, creating a rake angle greater than the fork angle. This modification shortens the wheelbase and makes the motorcycle easier to turn without sacrificing stability. As befitted the most luxurious touring motorcycle then on the market, the FLT featured the Tour Pak trunk as standard equipment.

This example is one of 1,636 FLT models manufactured in 1981. Mr. Bleustein donated the motorcycle to the Archives in 1999.

NUMBER 03 PRESENTED TO

Jeffrey L. Bleustein

COMMEMORATING THE RETURN
TO PRIVATE OWNERSHIP OF

HARLEY-DAVIDSON MOTOR INC.

1981 Nova Mock-Up

The high-tech, liquid-cooled, V-4 engine powering the Nova resulted from an engineering collaboration between Harley-Davidson and Porsche. This Metallic Gray motorcycle, assembled as a mocked-up touring model, is non-functional. For styling evaluation, many of the engine and transmission pieces on this example are made of wood. The actual Nova engine would have used an integral four-speed transmission.

This design study features an instrument cluster with a speedometer, tachometer, and clock, as well as tank-mounted indicator lights for fuel, water temperature, oil, and electric amperage. A low Tour Pak and shallow fiberglass saddlebags along with a cloth seat and passenger backrest pad hint at the Nova's touring potential. Engineers spent many hours in a wind tunnel, adjusting and refining the shapes of the motorcycle, fairing, Pak, and bags.

Engineering mounted the radiator diagonally under the seat. What appears to be a conventional gas tank actually houses the air box and electronics. Scoops in the fairing direct air into the air box. The actual fuel tank resides in a less conventional location, as indicated by the placement of the fuel filler cap below and behind the seat.

Only a handful of prototypes were assembled. No price was ever set for this model.

1982 Model FXRS Super Glide II

"This year we're introducing one more in a long line of revolutionary motorcycles. The FXRS Super Glide II . . . All around innovative design makes the FXRS the best-handling motorcycle we've ever built . . . The FXRS is clean and simple. It's not burdened with over-teched complexity. It doesn't look like a foreign bike because it came about in an entirely different way. It was built by people, for people—the way a custom bike should be."

—Harley-Davidson advertisement

For 1982, Harley-Davidson introduced a new frame that tamed the vibration of the powerful 80-cubic-inch overhead-valve Shovelhead V-twin engine by using a three-point mounting system with elastonomer mounts that isolated the drivetrain from the frame. The FXRS Super Glide II was one of the first bikes to use this system. This Vivid Black example is one of 3,190 FXRS models assembled in 1982.

1983 Model FXDG Disc Glide

"We think motorcycles should be dependable, serviceable, and durable. Not disposable. That is our philosophy. Our motorcycles are shining examples of it. Each one is based on our belief in simplicity of design. . . . Even today, most of the routine maintenance can be handled by the rider himself.

"Further evidence of commitment to our philosophy is our V-Twin engine design. By today's standards, one of its most remarkable qualities is that it can be rebuilt—many times over. The number of classic and antique Harleys in showroom condition attests to that fact.

"Ask any of those owners if they think a motorcycle should be disposable. They'll all agree that it is a great idea for things like baby diapers. But any respectable motorcycle is far from that."

—Harley-Davidson advertisement

The FXDG model embodied Harley's philosophy of building motorcycles for the long haul. It sported a monochromatic paint scheme, with the engine side covers and transmission cover painted in the same burgundy as the fenders, gas tank, and console. This model got its name from the rear disc wheel, which marked the first use of a solid disk wheel on a modern Harley-Davidson. By contrast, the front remained a laced-spoke, 21-inch wheel. The 80-cubic-inch Shovelhead engine powered this motorcycle, and it still used the four-speed transmission. Designers added a bobtail rear fender and used a 1919-style logo on the gas tank. The motorcycle weighs 585 pounds. The company manufactured 810 FXDG models in 1983 and sold them new for $7,699.

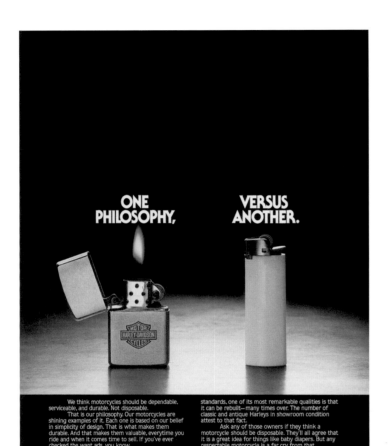

ONE PHILOSOPHY, VERSUS ANOTHER.

We think motorcycles should be dependable, serviceable, and durable. Not disposable.

That is our philosophy. Our motorcycles are shining examples of it. Each one is based on our belief in simplicity of design. That is what makes them durable. And that makes them valuable, everytime you ride and when it comes time to sell. If you've ever checked the want ads, you know.

Another reason Harley-Davidson® motorcycles hold their value is because we've held our ground. We've stuck to the basic ideas set forth by our founders 80 years ago. True, our motorcycles have become more sophisticated. But not more complicated. Even today, most of the routine maintenance can be handled by the rider himself.

Further evidence of commitment to our philosophy is our V-Twin engine design. By today's standards, one of its most remarkable qualities is that it can be rebuilt—many times over. The number of classic and antique Harleys in showroom condition attest to that fact.

Ask any of those owners if they think a motorcycle should be disposable. They'll all agree that it is a great idea for things like baby diapers. But any respectable motorcycle is a far cry from that.

MOTORCYCLES.™ BY THE PEOPLE. FOR THE PEOPLE.

HARLEY-DAVIDSON®

Harley-Davidson Motor Co., Inc., P.O. Box 653, Milwaukee, WI 53201
© 1983 Harley-Davidson Motor Co., Inc. All rights reserved.

1983 Model XR-1000

"A new motorcycle," the advertisement announced. "By the race people. For the street people." In 1983, Harley-Davidson introduced the most radical XL-based twin yet: the XR-1000, a hybrid that was part Sportster and part XR-750 dirt-track racer.

Built around a Sportster chassis, this model used a dyno-tuned 1000cc engine with XR-style, specially ported, high-flow aluminum heads, racing valve springs, titanium valve collars, and twin Dell'Orto slide-valve carburetors fitted with XR-750 racing-style paper air cleaners. Advertised as the fastest stock Harley-Davidson ever produced, the XR's engine developed 70 ft-lbs of torque and 70 horsepower. To introduce the model, Harley-Davidson and dealer Don Tilley entered one of the motorcycles in the Grand Prix at Daytona, winning their class in their first outing. The stock motorcycles came equipped with dual 11.5-inch disc brakes in front and a single disc in the rear. Production models had the race team logo on the timing cover, and they weighed 480 pounds. The handlebars are flat-track-style bars painted black, and the bike has a speedometer and tachometer. The company produced 1,018 XR-1000s in 1983. This Slate Grey example sold for $6,995.

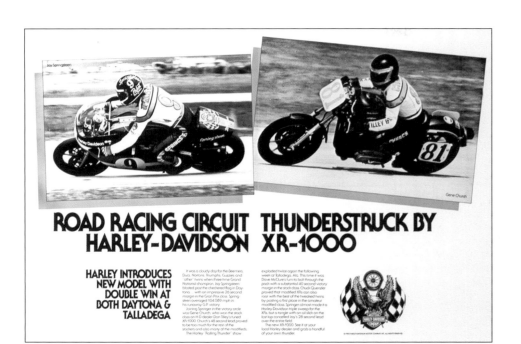

ROAD RACING CIRCUIT THUNDERSTRUCK BY
HARLEY-DAVIDSON XR-1000

HARLEY INTRODUCES NEW MODEL WITH DOUBLE WIN AT BOTH DAYTONA & TALLADEGA

It was a cloudy day for the Beemers, Ducs, Nortons, Triumphs, Guzzies and other twins when three time Grand National champion, Jay Springsteen blasted past the checkered flag in Daytona . . . with an impressive 26 second margin in the Grand Prix class. Springsteen averaged 104.089 mph in his runaway G.P. victory.

Joining Springer in the victory circle was Gene Church, who won the stock class on H-D dealer Don Tilley's tuned XR-1000. Church's 48 second lead proved to be too much for the rest of the stockers and also many of the modifieds.

The Harley "Rolling Thunder" show

exploded twice again the following week at Talladega, Ala. This time it was Dave McClure's turn to bolt through the pack with a substantial 40 second victory margin in the stock class. Chuck Quandel proved that modified XRs can also roar with the best of the tweaked twins by posting a first place in the amateur modified class. Springer almost made it a Harley-Davidson triple sweep for the XRs, but a tangle with an oil slick on the last lap cancelled Jay's 28 second lead over the entire field.

The new XR-1000. See it at your local Harley dealer and grab a handful of your own thunder.

1984 Model FXST Softail

"Of all the so-called customs being stamped out by other manufacturers, this is the one American custom that will short out their transistors. Introducing the FXST Softail. The Softail is a remake of a classic moving picture, the Harley-Davidson hardtail. Until 1957, the hardtail rear suspension was the hero of a free and adventurous American scene."

—Harley-Davidson advertisement

This 1984 Softail looked like earlier motorcycles with no rear suspension—the hard tails—but it featured a modern rear suspension with a rear swingarm thanks to two gas-charged shock absorbers hidden beneath the transmission, which provided the dampening for the triangular swingarm. To further the retro theme, the 1340cc Evolution-engine motorcycle featured a factory kick-start mechanism and a four-speed transmission. The motorcycle weighs 618 pounds. This Vivid Black Archives example is one of 5,413 FX Softails manufactured in 1984.

1984 Model FXRT Sport Glide

In 1983, Harley-Davidson introduced the FXRT Sport Glide, a radical new light-weight touring motorcycle that featured a frame-mounted fairing attached to the innovative new FXR chassis. The ABS plastic fairing was originally designed for the Nova project and had been fine-tuned in a wind tunnel. The following year, the Motor Company installed its all-new 1340cc Evolution engine in the FXRT. The engine had aluminum heads with steeper valve angles, as well as die-cast, oval-shaped, aluminum cylinders with cast-iron inner liners. Engineering fitted flat-topped oval pistons, having determined that oval-shaped shaped pistons conformed better to the cylinder when running at high temperatures.

The FXRT introduced an anti-dive suspension that utilized a two-chamber system controlled by air pressure and a solenoid operated by a brake-switch. In addition to the fairing, the FXRT featured a pair of side-opening saddlebags, and FXRTs purchased before June 1, 1984, received free Tour Pak trunks. Harley-Davidson produced 2,030 of the FXRT model in 1984, including this Candy Red example.

1985 Model XLH-1000 Sportster

"In the evolution of the modern street bike, the Sportster is the sole survivor. Since 1957, it has been the role model of street motorcycles."

—Harley-Davidson advertisement

The year 1985 marked the end of the line for the original cast-iron XL engine, which had remained essentially unchanged for the better part of three decades. Boring the cylinders to 3.188 inches in 1972 yielded a displacement of 61 cubic inches, or 1,000 cubic centimeters. By 1985, all Big Twins available to the general public used the aluminum Evolution engine, making this 1985 XLH-1000 Sportster the last mass-produced motorcycle manufactured in the Western world that still used cast-iron cylinder barrels

and cylinder heads. The 1985 Sportsters truly marked the end of an era.

Harley-Davidson motorcycles carried a "union made" label on a tag attached to the tube frame behind the front wheel for the first time in 1985. Sportster engines got polished cases, and the motorcycle used cast wheels, staggered dual exhausts, buckhorn handlebars, and a 2.25-gallon "peanut" gas tank. This Candy Blue example is one of 4,074 XLH models assembled in 1985.

1986 Model FLST Heritage Softail

"You are looking at a legacy fulfilled. The FLST Heritage Softail. It is more than just a superb factory custom bike. It is the embodiment of our entire philosophy: the most advanced engineering delivered with heart-rending style and grace. As you can see, it is more than a motorcycle. It will bring you back to life. It will allow you to fulfill your own destiny."

—Harley-Davidson advertisement

With the introduction of the 1986 FLST Heritage Softail, the Motor Company simultaneously took a step back to the past and into the future. This model combined the Softail chassis, with its concealed rear suspension, with a front fork assembly styled after the 1949 Hydra-Glide models. The Heritage Softail incorporated a chrome horseshoe oil tank, disc brakes front and rear, a drive belt, a powder-coated frame and rear swingarm assembly, a heel-and-toe-shifter, fender tip lights, lock-on directional signals and switches, front running lights, a pleated step seat, and floor boards. This example in Signal Red and cream had 10,828 miles on the odometer when Archives acquired it in 1996. It is one of 2,510 Heritage Softails manufactured in 1986.

1987 Buell Model RR-1000 Battletwin

A national AMA road racer and a chassis engineer for Harley-Davidson, Erik Buell left Harley in 1982 to build his own racing motorcycles. In 1985, Buell built a series of bikes using Harley's XR-1000 engine mated to his own racing chassis. By the time production ended in 1987, Buell had produced 50 of his RR-1000 models.

These bikes used the Motor Company's 998cc XR-1000 engine equipped with twin Dell'Orto 36mm carburetors, an integral four-speed transmission, and a Super Trapp stainless-steel muffler. Buell gave his RR-1000s full fiberglass bodywork and a front fender that almost entirely covered the front wheels.

Buell's frame consisted of a triangulated-geodesic configuration fabricated from 4130 chromium molybdenum tubing. It utilized an anti-dive suspension. The drivetrain was rubber isolated, using a three-point mounting system. The bike is equipped with a quick-change rear wheel, Pirelli radial tires on Dymag wheels, and a chain-transmitted power to the rear. The RR-1000 uses a 6-gallon Kevlar gas tank with a racing cap. The wheelbase is 55.5 inches, and the motorcycle weighs 493 pounds.

This orange and black Battletwin listed for $12,999 in 1987, but it was first sold for $11,000 on February 28, 1989. The Archives acquired this example in January 1999.

1987 Model FLHTC Electra Glide Classic Blue Knights Special

More than 20,000 riders hold membership in the Blue Knights, a nonprofit fraternal organization of active and retired law enforcement personnel who enjoy riding motorcycles.

For this group, the Motor Company produced a limited run of Electra Glide motorcycles in 1987. This Archive collection motorcycle is loaded with accessories that include a fleece seat cover, brake caliper and rotor covers, wide whitewall tires, S&S carburetor, trailer hitch, and many chrome parts and panel covers. This particular example, the first of 75 manufactured, has dual flags, red and blue pursuit lamps, and several Blue Knights decals. The bike has a police speedometer.

This example (in two-tone blue) had more than 100,000 miles on it when the Archives acquired it in 2002. Its previous owner had rebuilt the engine shortly before it joined the collection. During the rebuild, it received heavy-duty valve springs, reworked heads, titanium valve keepers, a stainless-steel cam and valves, a 32-amp alternator, dual coils, and increased compression (from 8.5:1 up to 9.0:1).

1989 Model FXSTS Springer Softail

"Now for something that'll really get everybody's attention. The Harley-Davidson Springer Softail. It's built behind a suspension system that hasn't seen the front end of a production motorcycle in almost forty years. But we did more than just resurrect an old design. With aerospace-rated materials and Computer Aided Design, this suspension is all new from the ground up. (Sorry, Japan, it's already patented.) With over four inches of stiction-free travel, it turns asphalt to glass. . . . If you've always wanted to send a message to the masses, make sure it gets through loud and clear. Put a Springer Softail in your favorite parking spot. And make a lot of noise just sitting there."

—Harley-Davidson advertisement

Harley-Davidson's 1989 FXSTS Springer Softail reintroduced the Springer front end, which Harley-Davidson hadn't offered since 1952, appropriately updated with modern design and materials. While the design hadn't been offered by the factory since Harry Truman was president, the springer front fork remained popular among custom bike builders, and its revival fit perfectly with Harley's philosophy of providing the style of motorcycle its customers craved. The company manufactured 5,387 FXSTS models during 1989.

1989 Model FLSTC Softail Super Bowl XXIII

"101 HARLEY-DAVIDSONS SET TO VAROOM INTO SUPER BOWL HALFTIME SHOW. NFL superstars won't be the only American legends to take to the field at Super Bowl XXIII on January 22 in Miami's Joe Robbie Stadium. One hundred and one custom-made Harley-Davidson motorcycles may well steal the show during what is to be the most visually exciting halftime program in Super Bowl history. The theme for this year's halftime show, 'Bebop Bamboozled,' combines the magic, mood and sounds of 50s and 60s rock 'n roll with the visual sensation of that period—3D. It is to be the first ever live 3D telecast and is expected to have the largest viewing audience of any Super Bowl halftime show."

—Harley-Davidson press release

So read a press release issued by Harley-Davidson on January 10, 1989. "The Super Bowl Harleys," the press release explained, ". . . recall . . . the classic Harleys from decades past. Only 107 of these. . . have been manufactured. Their specially designed graphics, which incorporate the Super Bowl XXIII logo, guarantee them collector's status." Of the 107 black bikes, seven remained on the sidelines as spares during the show because one of two all-white models, this particular example, filled out the program. The second of these white versions was the backup model. Following the game, all 107 black models and the other white one went to dealers for subsequent public sale.

In addition to white paint with red pinstriping on the gas tank and fenders and commemorative Super Bowl graphics on the tanks, the leather was white instead of black on the pair of white bikes. After the football game rehearsals, festivities, and other events, this motorcycle accumulated 120 miles before joining the Archives collection.

15

"If I Have to Explain...."

Evolution Era: 1990–1999

On February 24, 1990, magazine publisher Malcolm Forbes died at age 70. Besides a passion for collecting Fabergé eggs and dating Elizabeth Taylor, he rode and enjoyed Harley-Davidson motorcycles.

Forbes was just one of a multitude of Harley-Davidson enthusiasts who helped make the Motor Company the most successful and fastest-growing motorcycle producer of the 1990s. With the Evolution engine having proven its merit and a lineup of products that were exactly right for the market, Harley-Davidson motorcycles became the status symbol of the decade.

1990 Model FLSTF Fat Boy

"Just when you thought it was safe to go back on the street, along comes the new Harley-Davidson Fat Boy. Soft-tailed and hard-nosed. Ready to make an impression on all who see it. And move the soul of all who ride it. The Harley Fat Boy is totally different to anything Harley-Davidson has wheeled out of Milwaukee before. A new meaning to the words 'Factory Custom.' . . ."

—Harley-Davidson advertisement

To create the 1990 Fat Boy, Harley-Davidson started with a Softail chassis powered by the rigid-mounted, 80-cubic-inch Evolution engine and added a monochromatic Fine Silver Metallic paint scheme on the gas tank, oil tank, fenders, and frame. First-year Fat Boys feature yellow highlights on the timer and derby covers and on the center rocker-box spacers. Designers gave the bike a textured leather seat insert and a hand-laced gas-tank strap and seat valance.

This example sold new in August 1990 for $11,115. The Archives acquired this motorcycle with 9,887 miles on the odometer in 1996. The company produced 4,440 FLSTFs in 1990.

HOG WILD.

The New Harley-Davidson Fat Boy.

Just when you thought it was safe to go back on the street, along comes the new Harley-Davidson Fat Boy.

Soft-tailed and hard-nosed. Ready to make an impression on all who see it. And move the soul of all who ride it. The Harley Fat Boy is totally different to anything Harley-Davidson has wheeled out of Milwaukee before. A new meaning to the words 'factory custom'.

Shotgun-style dual exhausts, solid disc wheels and everything in bold silver on silver, set off by yellow hot spots on the new derby and timing covers, centre console, rocker box spacers and tank graphic. Then add a textured leather seat insert and a hand laced leather fuel tank strap to get a motorcycle that looks like no other.

All powered by the Harley-Davidson 1340cc V2 Evolution engine. There's no faster way to turn heads.

And for the owner wanting to create a Fat Boy like no other, there's a full range of Screamin' Eagle and genuine Harley-Davidson accessories just waiting to go into action.

The new Harley-Davidson Fat Boy. Investing in precious metal has just taken a whole new look.

Be sure to visit your authorised Harley-Davidson Distributor or Dealer to see the new 1990 model line-up.

NEW SOUTH WALES
Norm Fraser Imports Pty. Ltd.
Homebush
Ph: (02) 764 3421

QUEENSLAND, NEW ZEALAND &
NEW CALEDONIA
Morgan & Wacker Pty Ltd. Newstead
Ph: (07) 252 5691

SOUTH AUSTRALIA &
NORTHERN TERRITORY
Peter Stevens Motorcycles. Adelaide
Ph: (08) 212 1494

VICTORIA & TASMANIA
Peter Stevens Motorcycles
Melbourne
Ph: (03) 602 5833

WESTERN AUSTRALIA
Bikeworld Belmont
Ph: (09) 277 5388

BTB HD989

1990 Model FXRP

This 1990 FXRP served as a support vehicle for the Wisconsin Law Enforcement Torch Run for the Special Olympics. As such, the factory delivered it with the police speedometer, red and blue pursuit lamps, a siren, special saddlebags, and a Tour Pak with a rear strobe light. Normal FXR equipment included the fairing, front engine guard, tachometer, five-position rear shocks, dual front disc brakes, sprung saddle, heel-toe shifter, and floorboards. When Archives received this motorcycle in 1998, it had 12,959 miles on the odometer. It is one of 592 FXRP models with fairings that the company manufactured in 1990.

1991 Model FXDB Dyna Glide Sturgis

"If the latest addition to the Harley-Davidson lineup looks familiar, it should. We're proud to reintroduce the Sturgis. The look is unmistakable, but deceiving. Because underneath the black-on-black paint job lies a completely different machine. Five years in the making, the reincarnation of the Sturgis features an all-new steel frame, which incorporates forgings at major junctions. The new Dyna Glide chassis gives the Sturgis a look that recalls Harley-Davidson's original FX series. But that's where the similarity ends. Through the use of a two-point isolation engine-mounting system, the new Sturgis delivers a ride that has to be felt to be believed."

—Harley-Davidson advertisement

Harley-Davidson introduced the second coming of the Sturgis to coincide with the 50th anniversary of the South Dakota rally. This was the first of the Dyna Glide series and the first Harley-Davidson motorcycle designed from the ground up with Computer Aided Design (CAD). This new chassis used an internal steel frame with a single backbone that incorporated the two-point engine-isolation system while exposing the battery for a 1970s look. Forgings instead of castings joined major sections of the frame. Engineering mounted the oil tank under the transmission. Designers gave this motorcycle orange trim on the timer and derby covers, middle rocker-box spacers, and cast wheels. These motorcycles sold new for $11,250, and the factory assembled 1,546 FXDBs in 1991.

1992 Model FXDB Dyna Daytona

"Last March, Daytona Beach celebrated Bike Week's 50th anniversary. We decided to celebrate in our own way—we built a new motorcycle. Introducing the Harley-Davidson Dyna Daytona. A true limited edition built around our latest-generation Dyna Glide chassis, each Daytona wears a special serialized nameplate. Certifying that the owner is special, too. As in one of only 1700 worldwide."

—Harley-Davidson advertisement

To commemorate the 50th anniversary of the Daytona Beach rally, Harley-Davidson graced the 1992 FXDB Dyna Daytona with an Indigo Blue Metallic and Gold Pearlglo paint scheme, the company's first-ever production use of pearl paint. Designers also gave this motorcycle a special tank logo to honor the event. The bike was equipped with gold-colored cast wheels, dual disc front brakes, buckhorn handlebar, pillow-look seat, short sissy bar with passenger backrest, direction signals mounted on a lower clamp, highway foot pegs, and a chrome and black engine treatment. Designers set the speedometer and tachometer in the tank-mounted console and included cushion grips, braided cables, chrome fork sliders, and chrome switches.

This Archives example had 33,142 miles on the odometer when it joined the collection in 1997.

1993 Model FLSTN Heritage Softail Nostalgia

"What's the big hurry? Seems like everywhere you look, people are rushing around trying to get somewhere. We think people ought to spend more time going nowhere in particular. Making time for a little fun. Like the fun we had in designing the Heritage Softail Nostalgia. This is what happens when you grow up in America's Dairyland. The two-tone black-and-white paint scheme plays off the wide whitewall tires and the natural cowhide inserts on the seat and saddlebags. Sweeping back from the black-and-chrome V2 Evolution engine, the shotgun fishtails pour out a sound that can best be described as, well, mellow. And that is exactly what this Harley is all about. It's about an easy, black-and-white view of the world. It's about ambling around, going nowhere in particular. Nice, isn't it? Everyone else can just hold their horses."

—Harley-Davidson advertisement

The 1993 Model FLSTN Heritage Softail Nostalgia marked the only year the "N" in the designation "FLSTN" signified Nostalgia. In subsequent years it was called the "Heritage Softail Special." The genuine cowhide inserts in the seat and small saddlebags earned this motorcycle the nickname "Moo Glide" or "Cow Glide."

The Nostalgia sold new for $12,999. The company produced a total of 2,700 FLSTN models during 1993. Archives acquired this motorcycle in 1998 with 6,961 miles on the odometer.

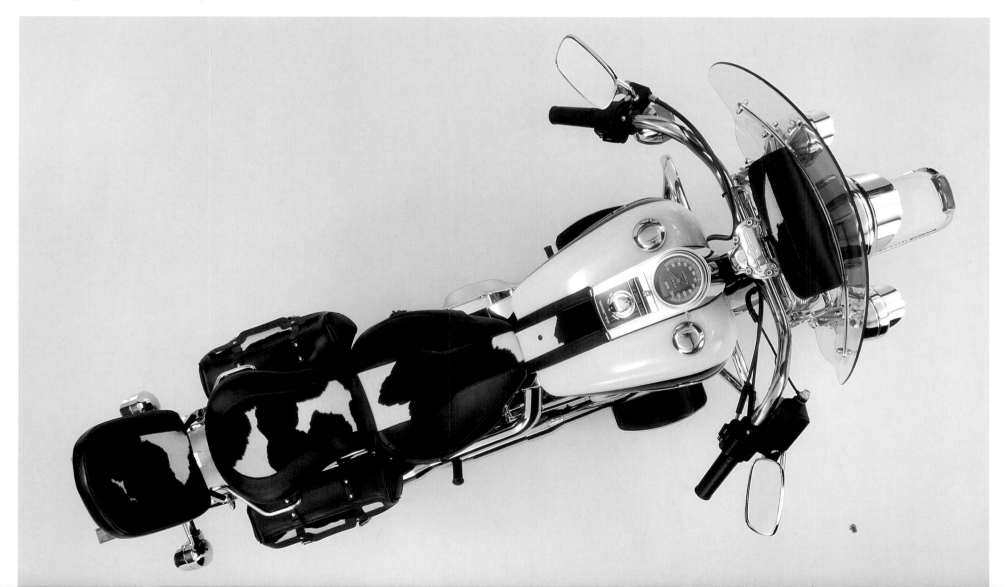

1994 Model FLSTN Fat Boy "Biker Blues"

In 1994, Harley-Davidson Motor Company commissioned Wyatt Fuller of Razorback Cycles to design and assemble this motorcycle to promote a new line of denim pants that the company was marketing. This bike appeared at all major motorcycle events and at numerous Harley-Davidson dealerships around the country before its retirement to the Archives in 1998.

The motorcycle was most notable for its denim-like paint scheme, complete with seams, stitching, zippers, and worn areas. Zippers appeared on the gas tank panel and the rocker-box spacers. Fuller's company molded many of the components from fiberglass, including portions of the frame, the rear fender struts, the taillight, the license-plate bracket, and a front spoiler. His fabricators also incorporated custom-made floor boards, air-cleaner cover, engine and transmission covers, ignition housing, and several caps and covers designed to resemble the snaps and hardware on denim clothing. Fuller polished the engine and transmission cases and gave the engine and wheels a denim paint treatment. Stitching on the custom leather seat resembled leather patches on jeans.

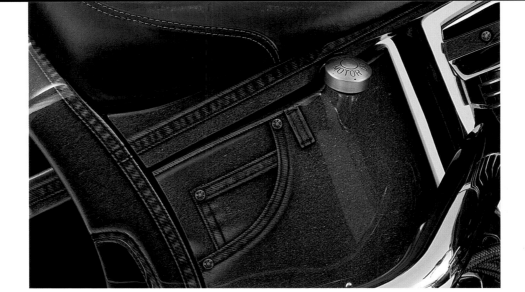

1994 Model VR-1000 Road Racer Street Trim

"Harley-Davidson is celebrating its 80th year in racing this year by competing on the superbike racing circuit for the first time. The VR1000, Harley-Davidson's new V-Twin road racer, is scheduled to compete in all ten 1994 AMA National Superbike race events. 1991 Daytona 200 winner Miguel Duhamel (pronounced Meeg-EL DO-um-el) and experienced 750cc Supersport and Formula USA Series racer Fritz Kling will be aboard the VR1000 for Team Harley-Davidson."

—Harley-Davidson dealer bulletin

In order to qualify for the Superbike series in 1994, the Motor Company had to manufacture a number of VR-1000 motorcycles for public sale and street use. Priced at $50,000 with full lighting and directional signals to satisfy AMA rules for the race series and federal regulations for street and highway travel, these motorcycles featured carbon-fiber mufflers, full fiberglass fairings and rear/seat fenders, clamp-on handlebars, steering dampeners, road-racing tires, monoshock rear suspensions, and chain final drives. Power came from 1000cc overhead-cam, off-set 60-degree V-twin engines. This particular motorcycle was assigned to John Baker, who ran the VR competition program for Harley-Davidson during 1994. After the company withdrew from the series, he transferred this bike to Archives.

1995 Model MT-500

In 1987, Harley-Davidson acquired the UK-based Armstrong motorcycle company, which was producing several military bikes using 482cc Rotax single-cylinder four-stroke engines with five-speed transmissions. Harley-Davidson used these engines in racing motorcycles, and the military market synergy made sense.

Built exclusively for military use—English, Canadian, and Jordanian armies, in particular—the MT has an electric start, chain drive, and oil reservoir in the frame, with high-tensile aluminum rims and on-road/off-road tires. It has plastic fenders and tanks, blackout lighting, guards for the hand levers, swiveling mirrors, directional turn signals, a high front fender with front-mounted panniers,

and a rear-mounted and enclosed scabbard for an automatic rifle. It also includes a third pannier, a luggage rack, long-travel front suspension, and a skid plate. The bike is equipped with shielded front and rear disc brakes and both a center and side stand.

The MT-500 offers 9.5 inches of ground clearance, weighs 370 pounds, and develops 26 horsepower at 6,250 rpm. According to Harley-Davidson literature, these motorcycles can reach 75 miles per hour, climb a 60-degree slope, and return 60 miles per gallon at 50 miles per hour.

1995 Model XL-1200 Biker Blues

In 1995, Harley-Davidson once again commissioned Wyatt Fuller to design and assemble a motorcycle to use in marketing for the Biker Blues jeans line the Motor Company sold. Starting with a 1995 XL-1200, Fuller installed many custom-made components, including the frame covers, front fender, air dam, left-side and right-side upper engine covers, air-cleaner housing, caliper covers, tappet-block covers, saddlebags, handgrips, shift lever, and clutch cover. The motorcycle incorporated a custom fairing, clip-on handlebars, two-into-one exhaust, bobtail rear fender, and Harley-Davidson accessory seat.

This motorcycle never was shown publicly. The company retired it in 1998 when it discontinued the Biker Blues jeans line.

1996 Model FLSTC Heritage Softail Street Stalker

"Unleash your dark side," the advertisement for the 1996 Harley-Davidson FLSTC Heritage Softail Street Stalker advised. Harley built this Street Stalker using a significant number of Harley-Davidson accessories. The company used this motorcycle as a show vehicle for its Parts & Accessories department. It was equipped with a Street Stalker Stage III kit, which included a rear fender, seat, taillamps and housings, dash panel, front fender, headlamp nacelle, front spoiler, 5-gallon gas tank, and side-mounted license-plate bracket. It used Thunderstar cast wheels, a Wide Rear Tire kit, a chrome rear sprocket cover, slash-cut mufflers, an oil tank kit, custom mirrors, custom grips, and a unique derby and air-cleaner cover. This Vivid Black example was transferred to the Archives in October 1999.

1997 Model FLSTS Heritage Springer

"The world is full of things that once conjured up mystery and awe, only to yield their secrets to science. And become boring. A Harley-Davidson motorcycle is different. While refined by modern technology, it will never be explained that way."

—Harley-Davidson advertisement

Harley-Davidson's marketing folks understood the fact that mythos trumps logos every time and that logic will never explain why riders wanted motorcycles that look like they were built in 1947 instead of 1997, the year the Motor Company introduced the FLSTS Heritage Springer. This retro-styled motorcycle combined the classic look of the Heritage Softail with the Springer fork from the FXSTS.

Equipped with wide whitewall tires, 16-inch laced wheels, sweeping front fender with running light, tombstone taillight, cloisonné tank emblems, dual fishtail mufflers, passing lamps, heavily fringed saddle, and leather saddle bags, the Heritage Springer's look transcended time. The FLSTS sold for $16,995 new.

1997 Buell Model S1 Lightning

This 1997 Buell S1 Lightning was Erik Buell's personal Daytona track bike. Heavily customized, it incorporates a reworked 1203cc Sportster engine with a five-speed transmission. This Thunderstorm version develops 101 horsepower with 10:1 compression and 90 ft-lb of torque at 6000 rpm. It uses a 40mm Keihin carburetor. Like all tube-framed Buells, the two-into-one collector exhaust system is mounted under the engine to centralize its mass.

Buell used this motorcycle as the concept bike for the 1998 S1, and it appeared in several magazine stories. It differs from the later production version by having extra carbon-fiber components, a racing seat, custom handlebars, a windscreen, and an instrument pod. After Buell finished with it, its subsequent owner added a custom-painted cutaway air cleaner, X1 aluminum rear swingarm, fiberglass chin fairing, 1996 front engine mount, stainless-steel exhaust header, carbon-fiber front fender, Thunderstorm heads and pistons, Barnett Clutch, Vance & Hines exhaust, Jagg oil cooler, and rear-fender spoiler.

The bike weighs 425 pounds. When Archives acquired it in 2004, it had 17,131 miles on the odometer.

1998 Model FLTRI Road Glide

"The Road Glide takes touring in a new direction. Notice the custom influence. It starts with a sleek frame-mounted fairing and low windshield exclusive to this motorcycle. Out front is an enclosed twin-oval reflector optic headlight. There's a unique new 'H-D' embossed seat and pillion, which accepts a rider backrest. The overall effect is pure custom touring."

—Harley-Davidson advertisement

This 1998 Model FLTRI Road Glide has optional Sequential Port Fuel Injection (indicated by the "I" at the end of the model designation). This was the first year for the FLTR model, which incorporated a new frame-mounted fairing with dual headlights, a gauge package, and a low windshield. These motorcycles were assembled on the FLHT chassis, and this series shared that frame, five-speed transmission, and running gear.

This example in Midnight Red and Champagne Pearl was a limited edition, number 46 of 800, with color-matched cast wheels. It sold for $14,850 new in 1998.

1999 Model FLSTF Fat Boy

This 1999 FLSTF Fat Boy was the first motorcycle Harley-Davidson assembled in its manufacturing plant in Manaus, Brazil, for the South American market. Plant managers used this vehicle to test the assembly process in the plant and then for certification runs in Brazil. This motorcycle was ordered to be destroyed; it could not be sold, since it was used for experimental development. However, the managers kept it and presented it to Archives in early 2003.

Built on the Softail chassis, the Fat Boy used the rigid mounted 80-cubic-inch Evolution engine with its five-speed transmission, marking the last time the Evolution would appear in a regular production Softail. In 1999, all rubber-mounted Big Twins had switched to the new Twin Cam 88 engine, and the following year the Softail line would switch to the counterbalanced B version of that same engine.

16

"We Ride With You"

Revolution & Twin Cam: 2000–

As the Harley-Davidson Motor Company's second century approached, Evolution-powered motorcycles continued to sell faster than the Harley-Davidson factories could produce them. It still seemed a new and revolutionary engine, but in reality it had been in production for nearly two decades, nearly as long as the Shovelhead and Panhead that preceded it and much longer than iconic Knucklehead. It was time for a new powerplant.

When the Motor Company developed engines to propel its motorcycles into the new millennium, it produced innovative designs that provided owners with everything they expected in a twenty-first-century motorcycle while maintaining the characteristics that had come to define Harley-Davidson motorcycles. The new XL, Twin-Cam, and Revolution engines exemplify the state of motorcycle engine art, but they are distinctly Harley-Davidson.

2000 Model FXSTD Softail Deuce

"You commit 4 of the 7 deadly sins just looking at it. Behold the cutting edge of Harley-Davidson styling. Pure tradition, in a place it's never been. Note the clean front end, stretched fuel tank and rear fender (Lust). Check the steel hoses, small turn signals and recessed taillight (Envy). The look would put a show bike to shame (Pride). At the center is a balanced, Twin Cam 88B engine (Gluttony). The Softail Deuce . . . The Legend Rolls On."

—Harley-Davidson advertisement

The 1450cc Twin Cam 88B engine powering the 2000 FXSTD Softail Deuce used the basic architecture of the Twin Cam 88 engine the company brought out in 1999, but the B version featured a new counterbalancer that greatly reduced engine vibration. Harley-Davidson used this new motor in all 2000 Softail models, allowing the Softails to retain their solid engine mounts while virtually eliminating vibration. The Deuce came with a stiffer frame, redesigned over/under shotgun dual exhausts, chrome oil lines, stretched 18.5-liter (4.89-gallon) fuel tank, and redesigned directional lamps. It added longer handlebar risers, new rear fenders and taillights, a sleek gas-tank console with a speedometer, new brake rotors, and four-piston calipers to the specifications list.

The Deuce left the factory with forward controls, a bullet headlight, drag bars, and a laced front wheel. Its wheelbase is 66.75 inches, weighs 644 pounds, and its front tire is a black-wall MH90-21. This particular Silver Pearl example was a styling department mockup that lacked tank graphics and striping. Styling transferred this motorcycle to Archives in 2002. Production versions sold new for $15,995.

2000 Model FLHR Road King

This 2000 FLHR Road King was one of just 16 identical motorcycles assembled under an agreement with the 2000 Sydney Olympics Committee, designating Harley-Davidson Motor Company as a "provider" to the Australian games. This FLHR was painted with a design called "Look of the Games," a color and graphics scheme jointly developed by Harley-Davidson and the Olympics Committee. The motorcycle was painted in Australia and features the Olympics paint treatment on the front fender, gas tanks, side covers, and saddlebags. The five-ring Olympics symbol appears on the saddlebags, while the front fender and side covers bear the 2000 Sydney logo. This motorcycle also has a U.S. flag and a Harley-Davidson flag on the rear. Original selling price for these commemorative bikes was $15,220.

2000 Buell Blast

This was the very first Blast that was assembled at Buell's new East Troy, Wisconsin, facility. Everyone involved with the manufacture, design, and engineering of the motorcycle signed the bodywork. It was a gift to Harley-Davidson's then company president, Jeffrey Bleustein.

The Blast used Harley-Davidson's first single-cylinder engine in 22 years, a 482cc four-stroke with a five-speed transmission. The engine developed 30 horsepower using a 40mm Keihin carburetor with an auto-enrichener, tuned air cleaner, header, and exhaust. The Blast used a uni-planar, rubber-isolated engine-mount system. This frame incorporated a single rear shock absorber, disc brakes front and rear, and cast wheels. Buell's engineers located the muffler underneath the engine and styled it to function as an air dam. The bodywork was molded in color. The wheelbase measures 55.2 inches, and the Blast weighs 376 pounds.

Bleustein donated this autographed Bulls-Eye Red motorcycle to Archives in October 2000. Original selling price was $4,395.

2001 Model FXDWG^2

"Let the gawking begin. The new limited edition FXDWG^2. A Scarlet Red paint job with gold-leaf flames finds the nearest set of eyes and locks on. A low-riding suspension and a color-matched powder-coated frame drop jaw after jaw. Tan leather seats with real ostrich inserts and a new full-length fuel console refuse to go unnoticed. . . . It's pure customized rolling spectacle."

—Harley-Davidson advertisement

Harley-Davidson's Custom Vehicle Operations (CVO) built this Scarlet Red 2001 FXDWG^2. It featured a color-matched fairing, chin fairing, frame, battery and electrical boxes, and coil cover. Styling accentuated the red paint with gold-leaf flames on the gas tank and fenders. This bike also had a full-length dash console, new air cleaner, slash-cut mufflers, LightningStar wheels and rear sprocket, a factory security system, low-profile rear shock absorbers, billet grips, custom mirrors, and foot pegs. It incorporated the Deuce turn signals and braided lines.

This motorcycle was equipped with a metric speedometer for the Canadian market. Original selling price was $21,995.

2001 Model FLHRCI Road King Classic

"Concrete is so temporary. A few things time will never wreck: the look of our front fender; the lines of our fuel tank; the sound of our engine. When we build a motorcycle, we build it for the ages. Dead set in our belief that what is right today will be right 50 years from now. In a disposable world, there's a lot of value in that."

—Harley-Davidson advertisement

This Luxury Blue and Diamond Ice 2001 FLHRCI Road King Classic was the two millionth motorcycle assembled at Harley-Davidson's York, Pennsylvania, plant. This Classic featured a detachable windshield, a hand-tooled leather seat, leather-covered hard saddle bags, a three-dimensional tank logo, wide whitewall tires, and laced wheels. The engine was the 1450cc Twin Cam 88. Road King Classic models sold new for $16,695. This motorcycle joined the Archives collection in June 2001.

2002 Model VRSCA V-Rod

"A lot of revolutions start with burning tires. It's a riot on the street all right, and there's a motorcycle behind it. A new mix of performance and pure Harley-Davidson custom. We call it the V-Rod motorcycle. Dragstrip-inspired styling. Our latest engine: the tire-smoking 115-horsepower Revolution V-Twin. In other words, the kind of movement we can all get behind."

—Harley-Davidson advertisement

Powered by a 60-degree, liquid-cooled, 1130cc engine using four valves per cylinder and sequential port fuel injection, the first liquid-cooled production engine in Harley-Davidson's 100-year history, the V-Rod represented a genuine revolution at the Motor Company. It was the most powerful street engine the company had produced to date; with 11.3:1 compression, the engine developed 115 horsepower.

The innovation didn't stop with the engine. The V-Rod utilized a hydro-formed perimeter frame, anodized-aluminum body panels, and an under-seat gas tank. The radiator had outboard-mounted polymer shrouds with vortex generators for maximum airflow.

This particular example was a pre-production model featured at the company's dealer convention and at the Sturgis show. It appeared in a television interview with Bill Davidson. Production models sold for $16,995.

2002 Model XL-883C Sportster Custom

Harley-Davidson Genuine Parts & Accessories painted and accessorized this particular 2002 XL-883C Sportster Custom for use as a display model only. Parts & Accessories mounted custom wheels, directional lights, seat, mufflers, oil-tank cover, "laydown" license plate, forward controls, tachometer, foot pegs, chain guard, mirrors, and headlight trim. Technicians mounted chrome controls, switches, and sliders on this motorcycle.

2002 FLHTC Electra Glide Firefighters Special

Harley-Davidson developed the Firefighters Special version of its 2002 FLHTC Electra Glide to commemorate the contribution that firefighters made in the events of September 11, 2001. Harley-Davidson manufactured 2,600 of these motorcycles, which were available to credentialed firefighters only. Once the buyer provided identification, the order was processed and the motorcycle delivered. Shortly after delivery, the company sent a special identification tag for the owner to affix to the vehicle.

The Twin-Cam 88 1450cc engine with five-speed transmission drove these customs. The bikes came standard with a Tour Pak, saddlebags, passing lamps, dual exhausts, and a fiberglass fairing with a radio and cassette deck. The instrument pod included a fuel gauge, voltmeter, oil-pressure gauge, and ambient-temperature gauge.

These motorcycles sold new for $16,560.

2003 FLHTCUI Ultra Classic Electra Glide with Sidecar

"The story of the century, Written in Steel. There is an epic story to be told. One of a hundred years of great motorcycles. Mere words could never suffice so we put it into chrome, steel, and paint. An entire line of once-in-a-century motorcycles."

—Harley-Davidson advertisement

After final assembly, Harley-Davidson had this unique 2003 FLHTCUI Ultra Classic Electra Glide dismantled and then shipped its individual components to all Harley-Davidson facilities around the world so its employees would sign it to commemorate the Motor Company's 100th anniversary. There are nearly 10,000 signatures on this motorcycle.

While this motorcycle represented an internal celebration of the Motor Company's first one hundred years, Harley-Davidson also celebrated with public events and commemorative models.

Regular production models of the Ultra sold new for $19,995. Once reassembled and displayed, this motorcycle made its way into the Archives collection.

2003 Model XLH-1200 Sportster

"Feel the brawny 1200cc Evolution engine come to life. Send the wheels in motion. Grin as the nimble frame leans in and out of turns. No matter what faces you at the end of the ride, this time is all yours."

—Harley-Davidson advertisement

This 2003 XLH-1200 Sportster was the last rigid-mount Sportster to be manufactured at Harley-Davidson's Kansas City plant. It used the 1200cc Evolution Sportster engine with its integral five-speed transmission solidly mounted to the frame. A completely new Sportster featuring rubber engine mounts would debut for the 2004 model year.

This 100th Anniversary Sportster came equipped with laced wheels with 100/90-19 front tires and 130/90D-16s on the rears. Its wheelbase is 60 inches, and it weighs 491 pounds. This White Pearl example cost $8,255 in 2003.

2004 Model FLHTCSE Screamin' Eagle Electra Glide

"Take a spin around the block. Utah, that's a nice block. The time has come for you to satisfy your appetite for a Utah-sized portion of the open road. Throw a leg over the custom leather saddle, and light up 103 cubic inches of Twin Cam bliss. You won't find a nicer touring rig than the FLHTCSE Screamin' Eagle Electra Glide."

—Harley-Davidson advertisement

Harley-Davidson's Custom Vehicle Operations (CVO) manufactured the 2004 FLHTCSE Screamin' Eagle Electra Glide in limited quantities. CVO used a 103-cubic-inch, stroked version of the Twin-Cam 88 twin, incorporated custom paint, and fitted numerous custom accessories, including chrome fork sliders, custom footboards, custom seat, touring mufflers, custom oil cooler, wind deflector, fairing-lowers, cruise control, premium sound system, and chromed handlebars with internal wiring, as well as a powder-coated engine.

The Screamin' Eagle Electra Glide weighs 785 pounds and rode on Detonator custom wheels. The motorcycle sold new for $29,000.

2005 Model XL-883 Police

Not every motor officer wants or needs a heavyweight touring bike. For those police forces needing something a bit more agile, Harley-Davidson offered the 2005 XL-883 Police model. This was the standard 883cc Sportster configured for police use, complete with black saddlebags, red and blue pursuit lights, an engine guard, a luggage rack, and a windshield. It weighs 555 pounds. The Birch White police model used a 100/90-19 tire on the front and 130/90D-16 tire on the rear.

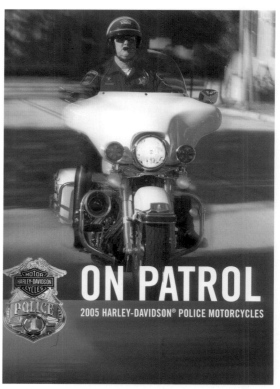

2005 Model FLSTN Softail Deluxe

"In 1903 William Harley and three Davidson brothers planted a seed in a Milwaukee back yard. What grew has since spread far and wide. Two wheels, an engine, and more than a century of wind and wanderlust have carried it along."

—Harley-Davidson advertisement

In 2005, Harley-Davidson introduced a redesigned FLSTN Softail Deluxe with shotgun dual exhaust, winged-logo tank, and 1939 paint scheme. This model got a redesigned upper fork cover, seat, luggage rack, and footboards. It carried over the 1450cc Twin-Cam 88 engine with its five-speed transmission. The motorcycle weighs approximately 670 pounds.

The Softail Deluxe models sold for $17,380 in 2005.

2006 Model FXDI 35, the 35th Anniversary Super Glide

"When Willie G. Davidson's Super Glide rolled off the assembly line in 1971, you could see it was different. Fat rear tire beneath a boattail fender. Narrow front end. Big Twin engine in the center. Gleaming red, white and blue paint on a one-of-a-kind shape. Thirty-five years later the Motor Company announces the Anniversary Edition of the Super Glide. Wide handlebars. Fat Bob fuel tank with dual caps. Loads of chrome parts. The famed #1 logo emblazoned on the tank, just as it was on the first model. Even the paint job does the original machine proud. Each of these limited-production bikes is individually numbered. Don't wait another 35 years to get yours."

—Harley-Davidson advertisement

The 2006 FXDI-35, the 35th Anniversary Super Glide, commemorated the 35th anniversary of the original 1971 FX Super Glide, a stylistic masterpiece that set the tone for Harley-Davidson motorcycle styling, appearance, and accessories for the decades that followed.

This motorcycle also introduced Harley-Davidson's new six-speed transmission, the Cruise Drive. It carried over the fuel-injected, 1450cc Twin-Cam 88 engine but received a unique silver-and-chrome treatment.

This example was the first of 3,500 to be produced in the Sparkling America color scheme for the 2006 model year. The motorcycle sold for $17,170.

2006 Buell Model XB12X Ulysses

With 6.5 inches of suspension travel, the 2006 Buell XB12X Ulysses proved as capable on unpaved roads as it was on paved roads. Buell powered the Ulysses with the Thunderstorm 1203cc, air/oil/fan-cooled, four-stroke, 45-degree V-Twin. Buell engineers mounted a fully adjustable Showa inverted fork on the front. For the rear, they fitted a fully adjustable Showa shock with a remote under-seat reservoir. On the front brake, a six-piston caliper gripped a perimeter-mounted floating front rotor. The rear used a single-piston floating caliper on a fixed rear rotor.

This Barricade Orange Ulysses example sold new for $11,495 in 2006.

2007 Model XL 1200N Sporster 1200 Nightster

"Is that thing legal?" *Cycle World* magazine asked in its April 2007 issue when it first received a 2007 XL 1200N Sportster Nightster for road testing. Referring to the low-mounted taillights, the magazine wrote that what it called "the toughest looking Sportster in decades" in no way looked like a production bike. That was intentional; in addition to the license plate being mounted on the swingarm, the Nightster features custom touches, such as unique paint schemes in colors like Silver Denim and Suede Blue Pearl, a hand-stitched leather seat, old-school fork gaiters, and chopped front and rear fenders. The Nightster weighs 565 pounds and sold new for $9,595 in solid colors and $9,990 with two-tone paint schemes.

2007 Model XL 50 50th Anniversary Sportster

This 2007 XL 50 Sportster commemorates 50 years of Sportster manufacturing and is the first of 2,000 assembled. The latest 1200cc, air-cooled, fuel-injected Evolution engine with its five-speed gearbox drove this machine. These anniversary models received serial-numbered nameplates with 50th anniversary emblems attached to the top handlebar clamp. There was an additional 50th anniversary emblem on the tank. A retro "H" logo adorns both oil tank and leftside cover, reminiscent of early Sportster models. The embroidered seat features the 1957 date in gold.

The other 1,999 commemorative bikes in this series sold for $10,000 each. This first production Vivid Black example joined the Archives collection in late 2006.

2007 Model VRSCDX Night Rod Special

The sleek, custom-looking 2007 VRSCDX Night Rod Special used Harley-Davidson's liquid-cooled, 69-cubic-inch Revolution engine and five-speed transmission for power. Harley-Davidson's styling team gave this motorcycle a black-on-black powertrain treatment with gloss black covers and a brushed, straight-shot exhaust with black caps and exhaust shields. This motorcycle has a 25.2-inch seat height and rides on a 240mm-wide rear tire on a slotted and machined cast-aluminum disc wheel. It has forward-mounted foot controls and uses a shorter, drag racing–style handlebar. Styling also redesigned the gauges.

Production examples of this motorcycle (in Vivid Black and Black Denim) sold for $16,495 in 2007. Archives received this early production model in June 2006.

2008 Model FXCW Rocker

"The FXCW Rocker makes an anti-everything statement that appeals to a hard-riding, go-your-own-way attitude," a July 9, 2007, press release announced, heralding the introduction of Harley-Davidson's most radical custom yet.

The new Rocker featured the design cues made famous by the celebrity chopper builders that populated the upper reaches of cable television during the first half of the decade, builders like Jesse James, Chica, and Billy Lane. This type of custom bike is often referred to as a "long bike," because of its exaggerated dimensions. As noted in the press release, the Rocker qualified as a long bike: "The Rocker stretches out on a 36.5-degree fork rake that extends the wheelbase to 69.2 inches."

To create the clean, uncluttered look of a bespoke custom, the Rocker used an innovative "Rockertail" rear suspension. The press release described the system: "It's the Rockertail rear end that makes a Softail a Rocker. The Rockertail utilizes an all-new rear section with elliptical tubes and no visible fender supports."

An enlarged version of the Twin Cam engine, the Twin Cam 96B ("B" denoting the engine was counterbalanced) provided this factory chopper's power. Prices started at $17,295 for a Rocker in Vivid Black.

2008 Buell Model 1125R

"Introducing the Buell 1125R: built from the rider down. The most important component on a motorcycle is always the rider. If that seems obvious, that's because it is. At least to us. It's why every decision made over the course of this motorcycle's development was based on how it would directly benefit the riding experience. The only innovations you'll find on the 1125R are the ones that make you smoother, quicker, nimbler or more comfortable. From its powerband to its ease of maintenance, it all exists for a reason. And that reason is you."

—Buell sales brochure

If a rider was looking for innovation, Buell's 2008 1125R had it in spades. From its perimeter front brake to its frame that doubles as a fuel tank to its rear shock that lies down in a near-horizontal position above the swingarm and frame, the 1125R is a sportbike like no other.

Even no other in the Buell lineup, thanks to its 1125cc, liquid-cooled, fuel-injected, 72-degree Helicon V-twin engine, which cranked out 146 horsepower and 82 ft-lbs of torque.

The 1125R has a dry weight of just 375 pounds and sold new for $11,995.

PHOTOGRAPHER'S NOTES

When I conceived this project, I planned to create a series of photographs that resembled those that I and others had done for the Solomon R. Guggenheim Museum book and catalog for their show *Art of the Motorcycle*. While Harley-Davidson has a photo studio called Harleywood, it was not going to be available to me for the three months that I imagined I would need to shoot as many as 225 motorcycles. I had to create a studio within the Archives Department.

The Motor Company's historic vehicle collection lives on the fourth floor of a building commonly known as "HDU," or Harley-Davidson University. About 470 antique, classic, historic, and modern motorcycles live in a temperature- and humidity-controlled space protected by a complex and intricate security system.

I designed a 12x16-foot stage that sat 1 foot off the existing floor and had a 20-foot-wide back wall that matched the stage color. Originally I had hoped to include a 4-foot-radius cove, but this projected the stage too far out into the available space, so it had to go. This stage had in its center a 10-foot-diameter electrically operated turntable that would support as much as 1,200 pounds, a figure I estimated was the weight of the heaviest motorcycle and sidecar combination we might need to shoot.

Triad, a local Milwaukee area exhibits manufacturer, created the stage to our specifications. They surfaced this structure with a washable Formica in the cream color I specified. Shoe prints and tire tracks that came from maneuvering bikes onto the turntable washed away easily with a weak mixture of chemical solvent available from Archives' restoration facility next door.

In an ideal world, I would have lit all the motorcycles using a large overhead softbox, say 8x16 feet or something similar, along with front and side fill. However two important obstacles—literally and figuratively—made that goal impossible. First, the motorcycle archives are located in a space that has only a 12-foot 6-inch ceiling at its highest point between 18-inch-deep concrete ribs. Electrical conduit and fluorescent light fixtures hang between and below those ribs. The second obstacle was even more serious: the entire 400,000 square-foot-plus building complex at 3700 West Juneau Avenue, Harley-Davidson's world headquarters, is covered by fire sprinklers. The company has its own fire inspector who visits every square foot of the complex once a week to be sure nothing blocks the sprinkler heads.

So a giant light bank wouldn't fit under that low ceiling, and I was prohibited from fixing Foamcore or Gatorfoam panels to the ceiling and bouncing light upward.

Here Loet Farkas of Advantage Gripwear in Atlanta, Georgia, came to the rescue. An internet search for parachute silk led me to Loet. My thought was to suspend the silk in such a way that each night we could drop it so fire sprinklers were not obstructed. But Farkas explained that the light loss through the silk was a great problem, as was the saturation through it from whatever color was behind it—in this case, an aged pale green paint. Filtering it would require extensive testing and cumbersome lens filter packs.

Farkas suggested a material called Claycoat, which provides 99 percent reflectivity and no light transparency because the "photographic" white is bonded against 100 percent opaque black backing. It is available in continuous rolls 5 feet wide, and he could install eyelets on finished ends. After measuring the distance between sprinkler pipes, I bought a quantity of 5x18-foot lengths. We secured three of these, overlapping them, to the iron water pipes that ran perpendicular to my stage direction. Using an assortment of bungee cords, we had a 10x18-foot pliable reflective ceiling that hung suspended between sprinkler heads.

Pliability was another crucial issue. My shot list for each motorcycle included one or more overhead views of each bike. But how would I accomplish this with a maximum 11 feet 6 inches clearance above the stage?

It took no time to track down a maker in Pympton, Massachusetts, Camera-Turret, Inc., who manufactures booms for smaller video cameras. I weighed the camera and all its accessories I had in mind and spoke several times with Lou Chighisola, who sold me a 12-foot Model CT300. By stretching it against the Claycoat, I could put my camera up to the ceiling right over the center of the 10-foot-diameter turntable.

I initially had planned to shoot this project using Hasselblad film cameras for ground-level images and my Nikon D2X digital cameras overhead. The D2X overhead worked great. I fitted a 6mm closed-circuit television camera to the viewfinder that looked straight through the camera eyepiece, and hardware connected it to a small video monitor at the operating station on the boom. The boom head gave me full pan and tilt capabilities with a wired joystick. A PocketWizard wireless remote trip fired the camera when I had the image I wanted; a second one tripped the strobes I used to light the stage. Nikon's 12–24 digital wide-angle zoom set at 18mm gave me room to spare on all but the longest bikes by pushing the boom up into the flexible ceiling material. Then I racked the lens back to 12mm for full-length coverage.

My original concept was to shoot 2 1/4 film on all ground-level images because I preferred the warmth of Fuij's Provia film to the neutrality of digital sharpness. But the digital images matched the Hasselblads in quality, and at the point when we reached motorcycles of the 1950s, when center or rear stands no longer supported the motorcycles, I put away the Hasselblads. That meant that for more than half my shoots, we used a scissors jack under center frame rails. Realizing that I would be scanning and PhotoShop retouching every 2 1/4 chrome anyway, the Hasselblads went into the bag.

Lighting was the easiest part of my planning. I have shot with Dyna-Lite strobes for more than 20 years now. I love their reliability, durability, flexibility, and portability. They offer nearly as much subtlety and finesse as more powerful, much heavier, and much more expensive systems, but I have shot food, fashion, interiors, portraits, and now 220 motorcycle shoots using these lights. To better manage color correctness on this shoot, I replaced every flashtube in my heads before I started. There is some evidence that tubes change color over their lifetimes, and I knew I had enough other challenges without having a dozen or more different colors of light.

To light my stage, I used four heads aimed up and slightly inward. To wash the backwall, I aimed one head at each side along the wall. This provided me with the light reflections I wanted on 3/4 views, filling in the sides of motorcycle tanks, fenders, and other sheet metal with a light tone. At the side of the stage and across each front corner at 45 degrees, I set a piece of 4x8-foot, 1-inch-thick Gatorfoam. These encircled the bike with reflective surfaces. I lit these front-quarter reflectors with one barn-door-equipped head per side.

I hung a second piece of Claycoat across the front of the stage from the ceiling and angled it back toward the camera slightly to fill in and provide a reflective surface for full-side views. To control spill and flare back toward the lens, I clamped four evenly spaced heads fitted with barn doors across the front of the stage.

On each side, I placed one additional head fitted with two snoots each (angle-reducing rings in Dyna-Lite's nomenclature) on low floor stands, and both sides featured a three-degree gridspot from Balcar. This provided a pencil-beam-like spotlight to rake across the front of the bike and highlight small details. My average meter reading across the motorcycle was f9.5 (including factors for the

polarizer), so I adjusted these gridspots to give me f11, just one-half stop more. I used eight M1000 watt-second packs and fourteen heads. Through more than 15,000 exposures, my Dyna-Lites never missed a flash. They worked flawlessly.

Why so many exposures? On film, I bracketed three frames at normal, 2 at 1/2 over, and 1 at 1/2 under. For digital, I shot a second exposure of every image in case one of the two files got corrupted. I downloaded flashcards to my laptop after each motorcycle, and in the hotel at the end of each day I reviewed each shoot. I backed images up on two separate external hard drives and two separate sets of DVDs.

Back in California, fellow photographers and friends Courtney Turner Forte and her husband James Forte followed

up my shooting with their PhotoShop expertise, removing jack stands and stage seams. In several instances, Courtney or James had to recreate tire treads, exhaust pipes, and frame tubes blocked by the jack. They and another photographer and friend, Rich Reid, created several levels-and-adjustments combinations that corrected colors to match motorcycles and the stage in every image. This became necessary because voltage varied throughout each day due to changing loads on the old building's electrical capacity.

For those obsessed with statistics, I shot 196 different motorcycles (plus 24 I re-shot for many reasons). I shot a minimum of 9 views of each motorcycle, but many of the bikes had 15 or 18 separate views. I shot 9,236 digital exposures that consumed 181 gigabytes of storage for each complete set of raw images. (I also shot 480 rolls of 120 Fuji Provia III before putting away the film cameras.) Averaging 30-plus motorcycles per week, we shot for seven weeks plus time to set up and take down lights, the boom, and the reflective materials.

Each day presented intriguing and fascinating challenges. It was an enormously interesting and enjoyable project. And it was the opportunity of a lifetime!

—Randy Leffingwell
December 2007

INDEX